THE BRI_____ICE

CONTEMPORARY POLITICAL STUDIES SERIES

Series Editor: John Benyon, *Director, Centre for the Study of Public Order, University of Leicester*

A series which provides authoritative yet concise introductory accounts of key topics in contemporary political studies.

THE BRITISH CIVIL SERVICE

ROBERT PYPER

PRENTICE HALL
HARVESTER WHEATSHEAF

LONDON NEW YORK TORONTO SYDNEY TOKYO SINGAPORE
MADRID MEXICO CITY MUNICH

First published 1995 by
Prentice Hall/Harvester Wheatsheaf
Campus 400, Maylands Avenue
Hemel Hempstead
Hertfordshire, HP2 7EZ

A division of
Simon & Schuster International Group

Typeset in 10/12pt Times
by Dorwyn Ltd, Rowlands Castle, Hants.
Printed and bound in Great Britain by
Biddles Ltd, Guildford and King's Lynn

Library of Congress Cataloging in Publication Data

Pyper, Robert.
The British Civil Service: an introduction/Robert Pyper.
  p. cm. – (Contemporary political studies series)
  Includes bibliographical references and index
  ISBN 0–13–354440 0 (pbk)
  1. Civil service – Great Britain. I. Title. II. Series:
Contemporary political studies series (Harvester Wheatsheaf
(Publisher))
JN425.P97 1995
354.41006–dc20   94–41280
                                                                    CIP

British Library Cataloging in Publication Data

A catalogue record for this book is available from
the British Library

ISBN 0–13–354440 0 (pbk)

1 2 3 4 5   99 98 97 96 95

For Emma and Michael

CONTENTS

PREFACE

The purpose of this book is to provide an introduction to the British civil service, combining factual description with comment and analysis. It should be emphasised at the outset that our concern is specifically with the *British* civil service, since, technically, the government of the United Kingdom is not served by a single, UK-wide administrative machine. The separate Northern Ireland Civil Service shares many common features and characteristics with the British model, but it is a distinct organisation, and does not form part of our primary interest.

The civil service is something of an enigma. For decades, its image was that of a rule-bound 'bureaucracy', staffed by distant, aloof mandarins at the top levels, and grey officials in the local outposts. The task of this predominantly London-based organisation was, apparently, to provide government ministers with impartial advice, steer clear of any whiff of political controversy and deliver services to the public while showing the maximum respect for regulations and jargon, and a minimal concern for the real requirements of the clients. Students of politics who took a serious interest in the workings of the civil service were likely to be deemed marginally masochistic, and perhaps a little like the subject of their interest: dull and a bit, well, boring.

This image of the civil service was a crude and misleading caricature. It stuck, none the less, and elements of it remain, even today. However, popular and academic perceptions seem to have changed to some extent over recent years. Perhaps this has stemmed from the political controversy surrounding the Ponting and Westland affairs, when the roles and responsibilities of civil servants became the subject of heated debate. Maybe the fact that a politically neutral organisation, designed to serve different parties as they alternate in government, has been required to serve a single party for so long, focused attention on the operation of the service. Alternatively, it might be argued that the Thatcher Government's much-trumpeted attempt to reform the civil service naturally created an interest in the results.

Whatever the explanation, it cannot be denied that the civil service today forms not a dreary backwater, but one of the mainstreams of political study. No longer confronted with a limited number of dated and dusty tomes, the interested student can now choose from an ever-expanding selection of general surveys and specialist monographs and articles. Newspaper, television and radio coverage of civil service affairs is surely greater than it has ever been, and the student seeking up-to-date illustrative examples should never be at a loss. As if the burgeoning academic and journalistic interest is not enough, the 'dull and boring' civil service has been the subject of an extremely popular and award-winning television *comedy* series (*Yes, Minister*).

This book offers an insight into one of most vital organs within the body politic, as it faces the challenges of the late 1990s. One of the major themes which runs through the text concerns the nature and impact of the structural and managerial changes introduced over recent years. Could these have the effect of dismantling the traditional, unitary civil service, leaving us with a looser, federal structure, characterised by organisational and managerial diversity? Can such a process take place without destroying fundamental elements of traditional civil service?

The introductory chapter will set the scene for the detailed examination which follows, by establishing some general benchmarks. The historical development of the institution, the key precepts which govern its operation and the basic conditions of service for officials will be described, before a few comparisons are drawn with the civil services of other liberal democratic states.

Chapter 2 explains how civil servants are recruited and trained, and examines the changes which have been introduced to the traditional, highly centralised systems. Here, we can note some symptoms of federalisation.

In Chapter 3, we turn to the overall size, shape and organisational culture of the service. The 'new' managerialism and radical
restructuring of the 1980s and 1990s are placed in context. An
attempt is made to distinguish between 'macro' and 'micro'
change, and the emergence of a federal civil service is discussed.

Chapter 4 focuses on the high politics of the civil service, and
considers the relationships between ministers and officials. The
roles and responsibilities of civil servants in the sphere of policy
are examined in practical and theoretical contexts.

The link between helping to create policy and playing a part in its
implementation is central to the functioning of a civil service. The
delivery, administration or implementation of policy forms the basic
concern of Chapter 5. Here, we look at the growing concern with
quality of service provision, and the controversial part played by the
Citizen's Charter in highlighting the 'quality' agenda.

The efficacy of the various channels through which civil servants
are held accountable for their roles in policy, administration and
management comes under scrutiny in Chapter 6. Consideration is
given to the extent to which the structural reforms introduced
under the umbrella of Next Steps have enhanced or weakened the
accountability of the civil service to Parliament.

In Chapter 7, the associated theme of official secrecy is discussed. The British tradition of relatively 'closed' government is
examined, before we analyse the implications of this for civil servants. Key case studies are considered, and minor changes to the
secrecy regime explained, in the context of the apparently limited
willingness and capacity of government to offer fundamental reform in this sphere.

Chapter 8 draws our attention to the growing importance of the
European Union for the British civil service. The rocky path to
UK membership of the EC is charted in order to establish the
broad context within which British officials came to work with the
European institutions. We describe the impact of membership of
the European Union on civil servants in a range of central, co-
ordinating bodies, as well as the departments and agencies.

The concluding chapter reiterates our basic theme: the emergence of a new form of civil service in the wake of the structural
and managerial changes of the past two decades.

I owe debts of gratitude to a number of individuals who, in
different ways, have contributed a great deal to the production of

this book. John Benyon, the series editor, invited me to write on this topic. Clare Grist, of Harvester Wheatsheaf, was all that one could want from a publisher: unfailingly patient, encouraging and constructive. Although I carry full responsibility for any flaws in the text, I am grateful to the anonymous reader who commented on the first draft of the manuscript, and to Dr Allan McConnell who took time during a busy schedule to read and comment on a version of Chapter 8. Thanks are due to my colleagues in the Department of Law and Public Administration at Glasgow Caledonian University, who contribute to an atmosphere which is conducive to research and writing. On the domestic front, my wife, Elinor, succeeds against all the odds in creating a quiet zone around the door of my study. Despite, the rather derogatory connotation of the last comment, I dedicate the book to my children!

ABBREVIATIONS

AA	Administrative Assistant
AO	Administrative Officer
CAP	Common Agricultural Policy
COREPER	Committee of Permanent Representatives
CPRS	Central Policy Review Staff
CPSA	Civil and Public Services Association
CSA	Child Support Agency
CSD	Civil Service Department
CSPCS	Civil Service Pay and Conditions of Service (Code)
CSSB	Civil Service Selection Board
DHSS	Department of Health and Social Security
DoE	Department of the Environment
DSS	Department of Social Security
DTI	Department of Trade and Industry
EC	European Community
ECSC	European Coal and Steel Community
ED	Employment Department
EEC	European Economic Community
ENA	Ecole Nationale d'Administration
EO	Executive Officer
ERM	Exchange Rate Mechanism
EU	European Union
FCO	Foreign and Commonwealth Office
FDA	First Division Association

FMI	Financial Management Initiative
FSB	Final Selection Board
GCHQ	Government Communications Headquarters
HEO	Higher Executive Officer
HMSO	Her Majesty's Stationery Office
IPCS	Institute of Professional Civil Servants
IT	Information Technology
MAFF	Ministry of Agriculture, Fisheries and Food
MINIS	Management Information System for Ministers
MoD	Ministry of Defence
MPO	Management and Personnel Office
MSC	Manpower Services Commission
NAO	National Audit Office
NUCPS	National Union of Civil and Public Servants
OPSS	Office of Public Service and Science
PAC	Public Accounts Committee
PCA	Parliamentary Commissioner for Administration
PQ	Parliamentary Question
RAS	Recruitment and Assessment Services (Agency)
RIPA	Royal Institute of Public Administration
SCA	Special Committee on Agriculture
SEO	Senior Executive Officer
SSRB	Senior Salaries Review Body
TSRB	Top Salaries Review Body
UKREP	United Kingdom Permanent Representative
VFM	Value for Money

1

INTRODUCTION
The nature of the civil service

If we are to approach a proper understanding of the civil service, we need to establish some general points of reference. The basic purpose of this introductory chapter is to set the scene for the detailed examination to come, by offering an overview of the institution, tracing its historical evolution, setting out the governing principles of the civil service and drawing some necessarily broad comparisons with the administrative machines found in some other states.

Who are the civil servants?
A working definition and overview

Civil servants work for the 'civil' as opposed to the military, ministerial or judicial arms of the state. Members of the armed forces, government ministers and judges are not civil servants. This is clear and straightforward.

There are large numbers of people, though, who are employed as officials in parts of the political system, and who perform tasks which bear some similarity to those of the British 'home' civil service, who are, none the less, not of direct concern to us in this book.

For example, although the 200 officials working in the Northern Ireland Office are categorised as part of the home, British, civil service, Northern Ireland also has its own, distinct, systems of civil service recruitment and management, and most officials working in the province are employed in a separate organisation. Our concern is with the British civil service, not the Northern Ireland Civil Service.

The home civil service also excludes those working in the diplomatic corps or overseas service, in the various departments of the Houses of Parliament (although the pay and conditions of these officials are linked to those in the civil service), in local government and in the National Health Service.

Our primary focus is, therefore, on those officials working within central government departments and their associated executive agencies.

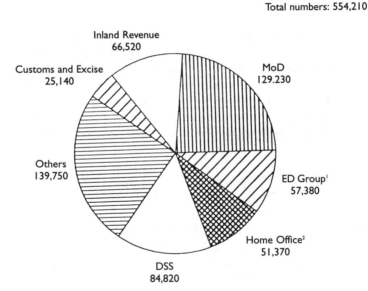

Total numbers: 554,210

Inland Revenue 66,520

Customs and Excise 25,140

MoD 129.230

Others 139,750

ED Group[1] 57,380

Home Office[2] 51,370

DSS 84,820

[1] Includes Department of Employment (with the Employment Service) (52,410); ACAS (620) and HSE/HSC (4,360).
[2] Includes HM Prison Service (39,000).

Figure 1.1   Civil service staffing by department, April 1993.
(Source: HM Treasury, 1993)

A brief survey of the annual civil service statistics allows us to sketch the outlines of a vast, heterogeneous organisation. Figures published at the end of 1993 showed that there were 554,212 civil servants in Britain, constituting approximately 2 per cent of the working population, and accounting for about 10 per cent of all public-sector employees (HM Treasury, 1993: 3). The government's expectation (Prime Minister, 1994: 30) was that the total number of civil servants would 'fall significantly below 500,000' by 1998.

Figure 1.1 shows the allocation of staff between a number of large departments. Only a minority of officials work in conventional departments of state: over 60 per cent are based in executive agencies, working at arm's length from their parent departments. A breakdown of staff working within executive agencies is given in Figure 1.2.

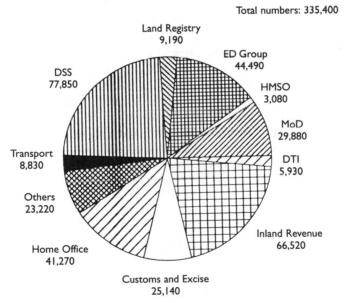

Total numbers: 335,400

Land Registry
9,190

ED Group
44,490

DSS
77,850

HMSO
3,080

MoD
29,880

Transport
8,830

DTI
5,930

Others
23,220

Inland Revenue
66,520

Home Office
41,270

Customs and Excise
25,140

¹ Including Valuation Office staff (4,960).

Figure 1.2 Civil servants working in executive agencies, by parent department, April 1993. (Source: HM Treasury, 1993)

Table 1.1   Civil servants by grade, gender and race[1]

Grade	Total	% Women	% Ethnic minority
1–4	1,070	8 ⎫	
5	2,950	13 ⎬	2.1
6	5,300	13	
7	18,100	18 ⎭	
SEO	24,300	14 ⎫	
HEO	80,300	22 ⎬	2.3
EO	122,800	46	3.9
AO	173,000	69 ⎫	
AA	91,100	71 ⎬	7.2

Note: [1] Figures are for the non-industrial civil service.
Source: HM Treasury (1993).

The size of departments and agencies varies considerably: for example, the Ministry of Defence employed over 129,000 industrial and non-industrial civil servants in 1993, while the Treasury was staffed by under 2,000; the Social Security Benefits Agency employed over 64,000 officials, but the Wilton Park Conference Centre, also an executive agency, was run by 30 people.

The stereotypical image of civil servants as Whitehall mandarins is distinctly misleading: only around one-fifth of all civil servants now work in London. Some traditional characteristics are slower to change, however. Table 1.1 shows that, despite some progress brought about by equal opportunities schemes and programmes of action, the civil service, especially in the senior grades, remains predominantly male and white.

Historical evolution

The civil service, like the monarchy, the judiciary, Parliament, the political parties, the Cabinet, the office of Prime Minister and the constitution itself, has developed in an organic fashion. A typical element of the British polity, the central bureaucracy of the British state was not created in a constitutional 'big bang' following a period of revolutionary upheaval. Instead, it evolved from fairly obscure origins, and was subject to decades of stagnation and decay, as well as periodic spasms of innovation and reform, and more controlled bouts of modernisation. The organisation which confronts us, as students of government in the late twentieth century, should not be viewed in any sense as a finished product, the result of centuries of progress. The organic development of the civil service continues, and more twists and turns surely lie upon the evolutionary path ahead.

An embryonic bureaucracy

While it is misleading to speak of a 'civil service' in British government until the nineteenth century, we can make out the beginnings of such a body in the administrative staffs of royal households, from Anglo-Saxon times onwards. Clerics, household servants and nobles of various descriptions provided kings with a range of services: record-keeping, military planning, treasury (i.e. looking after the royal monies and other 'treasures'), political advice and household husbandry.

The increased centralisation of authority brought about under the Normans, coupled with the gradual ending of the peripatetic court, led to royal offices and prototype departments settling in Whitehall. However, at this stage, the royal household remained the focus of administrative activity (Hennessy, 1989a: 18–20).

As the later Tudors became more distanced from the business of daily administration, powerful politicians-cum-bureaucrats such as Thomas Wolsey, Thomas Cromwell and William Cecil, emerged to oversee new administrative structures, at the pinnacle of which stood the Privy Council.

During the seventeenth century, a Committee of Trade evolved out of the Privy Council, and the Treasury (headed by five commissioners and a secretary) began to make its mark in the sphere of revenue-raising and financial control. By the 1780s it was possible to discern some traces of modern Whitehall as the old Northern and Southern Departments were transformed into the Home Office and Foreign Office respectively (in 1782), and the Privy Council's Committee of Trade was reformed as the Board of Trade (in 1786). The latter development is usually attributed to the efforts of Edmund Burke, political philosopher and Member of Parliament, who had spoken of the need for 'economical reform' in 1780, and sparked off enquiries into the financing and administration of government offices. The resultant Board of Trade was organised on the basis of a clear distinction between two government ministers and a small band of officials, and from this point onwards, civil servants could normally be differentiated from ministers on functional grounds. Despite the wide use of patronage and jobbery, flavoured with outright corruption (politicians could find official posts for their friends and relatives with ease), the convention of permanency was emerging. Thus, most officials would remain in post on a change of ministry.

Although a form of common pension scheme for civil servants was set up under the auspices of the Treasury in 1810, departmentalism reigned supreme, and the idea of a cohesive, unified civil service was vague, at best.

Northcote–Trevelyan, Warren Fisher and the corporate, unitary civil service

The organisation we would recognise as the modern civil service took shape in the period between the 1850s and the 1920s. In the middle of the nineteenth century, government departments were largely independent fiefdoms, recruitment methods varied, there was great scope for patronage and corruption, and favouritism rather than competence tended to be the main determinant of promotion. Although many individuals played a part in transforming this body into a corporate entity, based upon competitive entry and promotion on merit, the special contributions of Charles Trevelyan, Stafford Northcote and Warren Fisher cannot be ignored.

Trevelyan, having spent the early part of his career in the Indian Civil Service (an organisation greatly admired by nineteenth-century administrative reformers), was appointed to the top post in the Treasury, launched a series of reforms there, and argued the case for basic reforms throughout the civil service. He was particularly concerned about recruitment methods and the waste of talent caused by assigning bright young officials to tedious copying tasks. His evidence on these matters was not accepted by the Commons Select Committee on Miscellaneous Expenditure in 1848, but he had the sympathy of Gladstone. Soon after becoming Chancellor of the Exchequer, Gladstone set his political protégé, Stafford Northcote, to work with Trevelyan on an inquiry into the civil service (Hennessy, 1989a: 31–45).

The *Report on the Organisation of the Permanent Civil Service* (Northcote and Trevelyan, 1854) set out a charter for reform,

INTRODUCTION 7

which would not be fully implemented for decades (due to the innate conservatism which permeated some departments) but ultimately served to remould Whitehall.

Stripped to its essentials, the Northcote–Trevelyan Report recommended the following:

- A division of civil service work into superior, 'intellectual' and inferior, 'mechanical' tasks.
- Recruitment through an open competitive examination, conducted by an independent Civil Service Board.
- Promotion on the basis of merit.
- Inter-departmental staff transfers to facilitate efficient use of personnel and the creation of a more unified service.

These prescriptions for change were gradually introduced, often in the face of vigorous opposition from the Home Office, the Foreign Office and politicians from both major parties. The reformers were able to boost their case by citing evidence of the damage done to British forces fighting in the Crimean War by domestic administrative bungling, the demands from educational reformers for a proper career civil service to employ the products of the progressive public schools and Oxbridge, and the successful example of the Indian Civil Service (further modernised by Trevelyan's brother-in-law, Macaulay, in 1854).

Piecemeal, the fundamental changes took place. The Civil Service Commission was set up in 1855 and given oversight of a system of open competitive examination under the 1870 Order in Council. By this time, the functional division of 'mechanical' and 'intellectual' tasks had been implemented, and promotion on merit was steadily gaining ground. The Playfair Report of 1875 and the Ridley Report of 1886 endorsed service-wide staff transfers and a reformed grading structure.

Endorsement was one thing, implementation was another. It was not until Warren Fisher took the civil service by the scruff of the neck in the period following the First World War that a genuine corporate identity took shape, and the unitary nature of the organisation became clearly established.

Fisher became Permanent Secretary to the Treasury, and Head of the Civil Service in 1919, just at the time when that department's control over civil service matters was being tightened. An Order in Council, passed in July 1920, gave formal confirmation to a chain of events which had secured the Treasury's power over all civil service management and personnel issues.

Just a few weeks before, in a major strike against entrenched departmentalism, a Treasury Circular had given force to the Cabinet's decision that the Prime Minister would have the final say in the appointment or dismissal of all senior civil servants.

Throughout his twenty-year period at the peak of the Whitehall hierarchy, Fisher built upon these developments. He used his power to secure continuing Treasury dominance over the civil service, and to forge a more cohesive, unified organisation (Hennessy, 1989a: 70–4). He sponsored unity and the corporate spirit in minor ways, by supporting the creation of staff sports and social activities. More significantly, he established the idea that inter-departmental transfers should form a normal part of the middle- and high-ranking civil servant's career. This was secured within the Treasury by Fisher's requirement that all his own officials should previously have worked in other departments. Thus, although civil servants worked in a range of government departments, they manifestly belonged to a single organisation, with its own pay and grading system and common conditions of service. The civil service was a corporate entity. The semi-autonomous departments had ceded power, apparently forever, to the centre, and in this sense, a unitary organisational framework had taken shape.

The legacy of Northcote and Trevelyan was safe with Warren Fisher. However, Fisher's role as the guardian of the 1854 Report denied him vital flexibility. He narrowly interpreted the Northcote–Trevelyan prescription for 'intellectuals' to perform the 'superior' tasks at the top levels of the service as a requirement for generalist administrators rather than specialists or experts. During Fisher's period as Head of the Civil Service, the number of senior officials with outside experience and specialist backgrounds fell dramatically, while there was a continuing influx of Oxbridge arts graduates (RIPA, 1987: 16). This was to have serious repercussions, particularly since the whole purpose of the civil service was changing as the minimalist, 'nightwatchman' state gave way to *dirigisme*.

New roles and responsibilities in peace and war

Substantially increased government intervention in social and economic affairs became an established fact of political life in Britain largely, although not exclusively, as a result of two significant periods of progressive reforming government (the Liberal Governments of 1905–15, and the Labour Governments of 1945–51) and the two world wars. For the civil service, the new era of 'big government' had many consequences, some temporary, some lasting. These can be summarised under three headings: functions, size and composition.

- *Functions*: The role of the civil service in the nineteenth century was mainly limited to a number of regulatory functions, but, in the course of the twentieth century it was assigned a whole range of new responsibilities linked to the emerging welfare state, and the newly assertive role of government in industry. New departments and offices were set up to administer labour exchanges, the old-age pension and national insurance schemes, housing programmes and the National Health Service. Although state control of the key industries during the First World War proved to be a temporary phenomenon, as the private owners moved back into place in the early 1920s, a radical programme of nationalisation after 1945 left the civil service with a continuing role to play (at least until the 1980s) in what had become a mixed economy.

- *Size*: New departments and increased responsibilities brought more people into the civil service. In this context, the impact of the Liberal Governments' welfare reforms can be gauged by the fact that the civil service of 1901 had been approximately 116,000 strong, while that of 1914 numbered 282,000. War created demands for more officials: David Lloyd George became Minister of Munitions in 1915, and within months he had transferred existing officials and directly recruited new ones to build a new super-department of 12,000 civil servants: it was 25,000 strong by the end of the war (Hennessy, 1989: 61–2). During the Second World War, civil service numbers rose from 374,000 to 667,000. While there would be an element of re-adjustment in each post-war period, the general trend was for steadily increasing numbers, so that there would be over 1 million civil servants in Britain by the early 1950s.

- *Composition*: Both periods of war were to have a significant, but short-lived, effect on the composition of the civil service.

Businessmen, academics, scientists and 'experts' of various descriptions flooded into Whitehall as 'irregulars' to work alongside the career civil servants. The concomitant effect of fresh ideas, new modes of operation, more flexible approaches, as well as the enhanced role of technical specialists has been viewed in a generally positive light (Hennessy and Hague, 1985). However, Warren Fisher after the First World War, and Edward Bridges (Head of the Civil Service, 1945–56) after the Second, lost no time in re-asserting the primacy of the generalist administrators. The 'irregulars', and their methods, largely returned whence they had come.

The reformers arrive: Fulton and after

The 1960s brought questions of institutional reform into vogue as a search began for the causal factors behind Britain's sluggish economic performance. The civil service did not escape scrutiny in this period of self-analysis. Between 1966 and 1968, the Fulton Committee conducted a wide-ranging examination of the nature, purpose, composition and management of the civil service, concluding that it was 'still fundamentally the product of the nineteenth-century philosophy of the Northcote–Trevelyan Report' (Fulton Report, 1968).

The Fulton Report contained a series of recommendations which were designed to remodel the civil service and equip it to meet the challenges of the late twentieth century. The main elements of Fulton's prescription for change were as follows:

- Remove the strategic management function from the Treasury.
- Introduce management training for officials.
- End the 'cult of the generalist' and the dominant philosophy of the 'amateur' by showing a preference for specialists in recruitment and promotion systems.
- Rationalise the grading system.
- Enquire into existing methods of recruitment with the aim of widening the social and educational net.
- Restructure government departments by 'hiving off' some executive functions.
- Introduce new systems of accountable management, devolved budgeting and planning units.

The great majority of the Fulton Report was accepted, in principle, by the Prime Minister and the Leader of the Opposition. None the less, in the years that followed, its recommendations were introduced only selectively (Drewry and Butcher, 1991: 52–3), as political interest in civil service reform waned, and senior officials successfully neutralised what they viewed as the more damaging consequences of Fulton.

The Civil Service Department wrested strategic management of the service away from the Treasury, but its power was steadily eroded and it was abolished in 1981. The Civil Service College was established to provide management training, but most training continued to be offered within departments. While a new unified pay and grading system (the Open Structure) was set up to create more opportunities for specialists at the top levels, the dominance of generalist administrators continued. An attempt to integrate generalists and specialists throughout the service was thwarted. An inquiry into recruitment led to the advent of the Administration Trainee grade (for graduate entrants), but concern about the so-called 'Oxbridge bias' remained. Experiments were conducted with 'hiving-off', as well as new managerial and planning schemes, but these waxed and waned in the period until 1979.

Many aspects of Fulton's agenda were picked up by a new wave of managerial reformers in the 1980s. This time, sustained political support produced more substantial results, as fundamental restructuring of the civil service was combined with injections of 'economy, efficiency and effectiveness' and topped off with reforms in pay, grading and recruitment systems.

The structural and managerial reforms of the 1980s and 1990s were spearheaded by politicians of the right, who subscribed to the view that the civil service was the bloated and inefficient product of a discredited political settlement. The era of 'big', interventionist government, and the post-war consensus, were directly challenged by the Thatcher Government, which saw profligacy in every corner of Whitehall. The mode of operation, and the very purpose of the civil service, were being questioned as never before.

Curiously, only a few years before, the strongest challenge to the civil service appeared to emanate from the left. Polemicists portrayed the mandarins as Britain's new 'ruling class' (Kellner and Crowther-Hunt, 1980), emerging from a restricted social and educational background to dominate the elected politicians. Labour ministers including Richard Crossman and Tony Benn wrote about the innate conservatism of their senior officials and the ability of the civil service as a whole to deflect and neutralise radical ideas.

Whereas the leftist critique of the civil service found only minority support within Labour Governments, and little sympathy from Prime Ministers, the critics on the right were to find their views welcomed and fully supported by the occupant of 10 Downing Street after 1979.

Key precepts: permanency, neutrality and ministerial responsibility

The civil service which evolved from this historical process came to be characterised by its adherence to certain key precepts. It is a permanent service in the sense that it remains in place on a change of government. Ministers will normally be expected to work with the officials who have served the previous administration. Senior civil servants can be removed at the request of a minister, but this is extremely unusual, and will only happen if the Prime Minister and the Head of the Civil Service give their approval. In such cases, personal or managerial factors, rather than political grounds, are invariably offered in explanation for the change. A rare instance of a civil servant effectively being removed from his post at the request of a minister came in 1992, when William Waldegrave, the Chancellor of the Duchy of Lancaster, dispensed with the services of Sir Peter Kemp, the Permanent Secretary in the Office of Public Service and Science who had responsibility for the Next Steps initiative. The implications of permanency will be further discussed in due course, when we examine alternative civil service models.

Closely associated with the concept of permanency is that of neutrality. By virtue of the fact that they are expected to serve ministers of any political complexion, senior civil servants are required to be scrupulously neutral. The long-standing convention of neutrality was formally codified following the Masterman and Armitage Reports (1949 and 1978 respectively). Senior officials, and those working in ministers' private offices, cannot be candidates for election to the House of Commons or the European Parliament, nor can they hold party office, canvass for candidates or express views in public if any of these are associated with the politics of the UK or European Parliaments. Permission may be given for participation in local politics. Political restrictions loosen somewhat further down the hierarchy, and, in general, civil servants graded as Higher Executive Officers and below are largely free to engage in national and local political activities.

It is often argued that, in addition to its permanency and neutrality, the civil service is characterised by anonymity. This is taken to mean that officials remain 'faceless' figures, shielded from publicity by their ministerial superiors. In fact, the concept of civil service anonymity is extremely problematic. Officials charged with delivering services directly to the public in benefit offices or similar establishments can scarcely be described as faceless and anonymous. Not only are their faces patently on view, they are now clearly identified by the name badges they wear! Even in the upper reaches of the service, it must be doubtful whether facelessness and anonymity ever characterised the activities of Warren Fisher, Edward Bridges and their successors: they were and are public figures. The activities of House of Commons select committees, which take evidence in public from senior officials as a matter of course, have further eroded this particular feature of the civil service.

We cannot, therefore, take the concepts of facelessness and anonymity too literally. If they have any meaning, they refer to the less tangible consequences of the doctrine of individual ministerial responsibility. This constitutional doctrine serves many purposes: it can help us to understand the various roles performed by government ministers and the extent to which they can be held accountable in Parliament for the work of their departments (and for their own actions). Although commonly associated with resignations, individual ministerial responsibility is, in fact, much more than a charter for the imposition of sanctions on erring politicians (Pyper, 1987a).

Viewed simplistically, as it so often is, the doctrine tells us that it is ministers, not civil servants, who are accountable to Parliament for the work of government departments, and, correspondingly, it is ministers who must take the blame when things go wrong. In Chapter 6, it will become clear that civil servants are far from immune from the demands of parliamentary accountability, and the advent of the Next Steps executive agencies have simply added a new dimension to the whole question of official accountability.

The idea that ministers shield their civil servants from blame when things go wrong is seriously flawed. In the aftermath of the celebrated, and greatly misunderstood, Crichel Down case, during which officials had been identified with erroneous policy implementation, the Home Secretary, Sir David Maxwell Fyfe, attempted to set out the respective positions of ministers and civil servants (Maxwell Fyfe, 1954). In cases of error, ministers should 'protect and defend' officials who had acted in accordance with the explicit instructions of, or the broad guidelines laid down by, their political masters. Where officials had acted without clear ministerial approval, or in areas where ministers could not have been expected to hold much detailed knowledge, the latter would only be expected to answer questions about the chain of events.

Maxwell Fyfe's informal guidelines broke down in the wake of the Vehicle and General affair in 1972. The collapse of this large insurance company, and the apparent negligence of the Department of Trade and Industry, provoked a public outcry. The Secretary of State seized upon a seriously flawed official report (the James Report) as the basis for his argument that ministers were not to blame: the buck was effectively passed to a single civil servant who was publicly named and blamed for the department's failure to act in advance of Vehicle and General's collapse (Baker, 1972). This was despite the fact that the insurance company's imminent collapse had been the subject of informed comment for months, and was hardly a matter for which ministers could not have been expected to hold detailed knowledge.

At this point, another Home Secretary, Reginald Maudling offered his own interpretation of how culpability should be apportioned between ministers and civil servants:

> Ministers are responsible to Parliament still for all the actions of their Departments. A Minister takes any praise for anything good that his Department does. He must take the blame for anything bad that it does. That is a simple principle. A Minister cannot say in this House 'I'm sorry. We made a mess of it. It was not my fault. Mr So-and-So, the assistant secretary got it wrong that day.' One cannot do that. (Maudling, 1972: col. 159)

Maudling did not feel able to carry this argument through to its logical conclusion in relation to Vehicle and General, however, and he ended by maintaining that ministers should not be blamed in that case!

It has become obvious that formulations in the mould of Maxwell Fyfe and Maudling are quickly set aside when political careers are at risk: thus, for example, the naming and blaming of prison officers, Home Office and Northern Ireland Office civil servants for the escapes by Irish Republican prisoners from the Maze Prison in 1983 and Brixton Prison in 1991 (Pyper, 1992). Again, ministers hid behind the conclusions of official reports (the Hennessy Report in 1984, the Tumim Report in 1991) which blamed the escapes on administrative, managerial or operational failings, while ignoring the overall responsibility of ministers for such matters. Furthermore, in the Brixton case, there was some evidence of policy failure, which the Tumim Report ignored.

In brief, when seeking guidance on the meaning and impact of individual ministerial responsibility for the civil service, we should treat the statements of politicians and constitutional pundits with some caution and look instead to the lessons of key case studies!

Conditions of service

Beyond the general principles of permanency and neutrality, and the doctrine of individual ministerial responsibility, we can offer some broad comments at this stage about some of the more specific conditions of service which apply to officials. It should be borne in mind that many of the themes considered here will be developed later in the book.

Three key aspects of any discussion of conditions of service will be examined in turn: the place of the trade unions, the issue of pay and rules of conduct.

Trade unions

Civil servants are represented by a range of trade unions, the seven most significant of which are affiliated to the Council of Civil Service Unions. Numerically strongest are the Civil and Public Services Association (CPSA) and the National Union of Civil and Public Servants (NUCPS), which represent lower and middle managers as well as support staff such as cleaners, messengers and telephonists. Prison officers, Inland Revenue staff and civil servants in Northern Ireland have their own unions, while professionals, scientists and other specialists belong to the Institute of Professional Civil Servants (IPCS). Higher-level managers are represented by the First Division Association (FDA).

In general terms, over the period since the early 1970s, there has been a decline in the traditional convention of quiet negotiation between government and unions (through the medium of the Whitley Councils), and an increase in confrontation.

The first civil service strike took place in 1973. Six years later there was a nine-week pay dispute which resulted in a clear victory for the unions. Another major pay dispute broke out in 1981, during which union members at the Government Communications Headquarters (GCHQ) in Cheltenham joined their colleagues elsewhere in the civil service in taking strike action. At the end of the dispute, the government and the unions began to negotiate an agreement which would prevent future strikes by the type of security and intelligence workers based at GCHQ. However, in December 1983, with the negotiations still going on, the government acted without warning to ban trade union membership among GCHQ staff (the announcement was made to the House of Commons in January 1984). This decision, which surprised many senior ministers as well as the unions, precipitated a long legal battle, at the end of which the government emerged victorious. However, the GCHQ case polarised the relationship between the government and the civil service unions, and marked the beginning of a period when unions openly questioned and campaigned against many aspects of the government's management of the civil service. A prime illustration of this came in November 1993, when over a quarter of a million civil servants staged a one-day strike against the government's market testing programme (which involved the possible contracting-out of thousands of jobs).

Pay

By the early 1990s the entire system of civil service pay had started to change from a traditional scheme of national bargaining based around incremental scales linked to the service grading structure, to one characterised by increasing diversity, flexibility and moves towards local bargaining.

The major factors behind this change were the general economic pressures on government which created demands for tight control of the Public Sector Borrowing Requirement, coupled with a drive to introduce new managerial techniques throughout the civil service. The latter involved, among other things, giving managers greater control over salary bills, building 'flexibilities' into the pay scales in order to attract fresh talent into the civil service and encouraging the introduction of performance-related pay. The Civil Service (Management Functions) Act of 1993 delegated responsibility for pay and pay-related conditions of employment from the Treasury to individual Secretaries of State. By the summer of 1994, around 60 per cent of the civil service had gone over to a system of local (i.e. department- or agency-based) pay bargaining, and the government's aim was for the total replacement of national pay arrangements by 1996 (Prime Minister, 1994: 26).

From August 1993, even those officials working in departments or agencies which had not yet taken full delegated powers over pay schemes were being paid on a new basis. The old incremental scales were abolished, and each official was placed on a point within a new 'pay range' for his or her grade. A 'standard increase' would be negotiated between the unions and the Treasury each year, and this would be paid to all officials with the exception of those whose performance had been assessed in their annual staff reports as 'less than fully satisfactory'. Individuals could move up the pay range only if their performance merited it: a special budget would be paid to departments in order to allow them to make the performance-related payments.

While the trade unions had serious concerns about the impact of the new system upon their members, they came to realise that the government was determined to introduce this major reform, and concentrated on obtaining as many concessions as possible. One example here was the agreement that performance criteria should be negotiated between departments and unions, rather than simply left to the departments themselves.

The system for reviewing the salaries of the most senior civil servants (ranked Under Secretary and above) remained largely unchanged for an extended period following reform in 1971. These were considered, along with those in the upper reaches of the judiciary and the armed forces, by the Senior Salaries Review Body (SSRB – formerly the Top Salaries Review Body or TSRB). The recommendations of the SSRB are considered by the government, but they are not invariably accepted. In 1985, the Thatcher

Government had to fend off a revolt in the House of Commons when it accepted the TSRB recommendation that top salaries should rise by an average of 46 per cent. The Major Government rejected the TSRB's advice in July 1992, and held the salary increase to 4 per cent, rather than the recommended 25 per cent (thus, a Permanent Secretary's salary rose from £84,250 to £87,620, not to the recommended £100,000). Of course, as we shall see, the salaries of most Chief Executives of the new agencies were short-term (renewable after three years in most cases) and performance-related, and elements of this system spread into the senior open structure. In particular, performance-related pay became the norm for grades below Permanent Secretary.

In 1994, the government announced its intention to introduce greater flexibility in the pay system for senior civil servants (Prime Minister, 1994: 44–5). While the Senior Salaries Review Body would continue to advise on the overall ranges for rates of pay, the salaries of all officials in the top five grades of the service would be determined by the nature of the responsibilities they exercised. Accordingly, the central grading structure would be abolished, and key decisions about the position of individual civil servants within the pay ranges would be taken by a renumeration committee (for Permanent Secretaries) and Permanent Secretaries (for senior departmental staff).

Conduct

There are many detailed ethical issues linked to the conduct of civil servants and their conditions of service (including the dilemma posed by crises of conscience, and the matter of open government and official secrecy) which will be examined more appropriately in Chapter 7. For the time being, it will be sufficient to set out the basic framework of rules governing conduct.

We have already examined the restrictions which apply to civil servants in relation to political activities. These rules were formerly set out in the Civil Service Pay and Conditions of Service (CSPCS) Code and the Establishment Officers' Guide, together with others relating to the acceptance of gifts, rewards, awards and prizes; the procedures for reporting bankruptcy, insolvency, arrests or convictions; and the holding of shares or directorships. Beginning in 1993, the six volumes of the CSPCS Code and the

Establishment Officers' Guide were gradually replaced by the Civil Service Management Code, a much slimmer document, which simply sets out the general rules and principles to be followed by departments and agencies when producing their own staff handbooks. Once again, the watchword is decentralisation: much greater discretion over standards of conduct and discipline would be given to managers in departments and agencies. The new Code, which came fully into effect in January 1994, takes account of increased management flexibilities. It is designed to form the basis for a further bout of decentralisation, whereby individual departments and agencies will produce their own staff handbooks.

The civil servant's duties of loyalty to the government, and lifelong confidentiality, are reiterated in the new Code, despite the major controversies provoked by these issues in the 1980s (see Chapter 7) and without regard to the attempts of the First Division Association to have a 'Code of Ethics' drawn up for civil servants. Similarly, no serious account was taken of the debate surrounding the 'revolving door' syndrome of post-retirement jobs for senior officials within private companies which are clients of government departments (see Chapter 4).

A comparative perspective

Our remaining introductory task is briefly to set the British civil service within a wider context. What are the fundamental similarities and differences between the British civil service and those to be found in other states?

International comparisons, focusing on the civil services of liberal democratic states, reveal a range of basic similarities (Kingdom, 1990a; Page, 1992). The first of these relates to the role of a civil service in the policy sphere. In 1887, the American academic, later President, Woodrow Wilson, tried to differentiate between the spheres of politics and public administration. He claimed that professional administrators stood apart from politics, and their function was to implement policies in a totally impartial fashion (Wilson, 1887). Public administration was a respectable career, quite distinct from the crude world of politics. Wilson's motives were sound: he was attempting to save administrators from the open corruption of late nineteenth-century American politics.

However, his thesis represented neither an accurate description of the real world of government, nor a sensible proposal for reform.

By its very nature, the work of civil servants in liberal democratic states involves participation in the political process. Officials provide policy advice to politicians, implement the agreed policies of governments, and play their part in the systems of political accountability and control which exist to check upon the actions of government. While there may be debates and arguments regarding the demarcation lines between ministerial and official responsibility for these activities, it cannot be denied that in each sphere civil servants make judgements which are tinged with political considerations. They may not be party politicians, but neither are they political geldings. The world of public administration in which civil servants operate is not a politically neutered environment: this much is true of Britain and comparable liberal democracies.

A second fundamental similarity between the British and other civil services in liberal democratic states relates to some of the characteristics of the senior officials. To a significant extent, top civil servants form an elite, in the sense that they tend to be drawn from a relatively narrow educational and social base. There is an international variation upon the British 'Oxbridge factor'. Thus, for example, the French *grands corps*, emanating mainly from the Ecole Nationale d'Administration (ENA), and the propensity for the middle-class products of certain schools and universities to be disproportionately represented in the upper echelons of civil services throughout the western world.

A third similarity relates to the management of civil services. Across the liberal democracies, it is possible to perceive an increasing trend towards the adoption of private-sector managerial techniques, often combined with a tendency to utilise semi-autonomous agencies, rather than monolithic departments, for the execution of public policy. In some states, such as Sweden, the use of such agencies is a long-established feature of the government machine (Jones, 1990), while in others, including Britain, experiments with agencies have ebbed and flowed over the years.

So far, so similar. However, when we turn our attention to the means by which officials are appointed to top posts, a potentially significant distinguishing feature emerges. It is often asserted that the British civil service differs from those to be found in some other states by virtue of its system of promotion by merit. The career civil service can be contrasted with a politicised 'spoils' system, in which senior civil service appointments are in the power of politicians from the party of government.

In fact, when we compare Britain and other liberal democracies, we discover shades of grey, rather than bold black and white distinctions. Britain, and most other states, have senior civil services which are not openly politicised. As we shall see in Chapter 2, Britain has slowly moved away from a predominantly closed entry system, wherein the vast majority of senior civil servants were recruited by means of competitive examination and progressed up the hierarchy on the basis of merit. Instead, what can be described as a modified lateral entry system is emerging. Many senior posts are now open to outsiders in the sense that vacancies can be advertised and external, non-civil-service candidates can be considered. The modified lateral entry system can be differentiated from the type of full-blooded, unrestricted lateral entry system to be found in Canada, for example, where there 'is a tradition that a substantial proportion of the upper echelons of the service is recruited from outside the service; from industry, commerce, and the academic establishment' (Kingdom, 1990b: 48). While there are distinctions to be made among Britain's traditional closed, career and merit system, our more recent modified lateral entry system, and the unrestricted lateral entry system, more fundamental differences exist between all of these on the one hand and the politicised 'spoils' system on the other.

The United States offers us the clearest example of a 'spoils' system within a liberal democracy. None the less, on close examination, it is obvious that the American civil service is something of a hybrid, since it combines elements of the merit and 'spoils' systems. Since the nineteenth century, the US civil service has evolved

> from one in which jobs at all levels were used to repay political friends to one in which people believed to be politically friendly are enlisted in the higher levels of the administration in the attempt to strengthen the impact of the President upon the executive branch. (Page, 1992: 28–9)

Although confusion regarding the classification of certain posts makes precision very difficult, it has been estimated that over 90 per cent of federal government employees are career officials, with approximately 200,000 posts allocated on the basis of political patronage (Chandler, 1990: 165). However, only around 2,000–3,000 posts are filled by appointees who are obliged to resign when a President ends his term in office (Page, 1992: 35). Thus, the greater part of the US civil service is a career service, governed by the principle of promotion on merit. However, at the top levels, officials are nominated by, or in the name of, a President, and the cream of these will leave their posts at the end of the presidential term in office. Political appointees can also be found in some posts similar to those occupied by career officials in other departments or agencies.

The major advantage this brings is the provision of committed support for the policies and style of the President in key positions. This must be measured against the tendency of even a limited 'spoils' system to damage morale in the career bureaucracy (why strive for perfection if most of the top jobs will remain beyond one's reach?), cause substantial disruption to the process of government while appointments are made by a new President and the new people 'learn the ropes', and run the risk of corrupt or inappropriate appointments.

Having outlined the main features of the British civil service, let us now turn our attention to the key issue of recruitment and training.

2

MANDARINS AND MANAGERS
Recruitment and training

The introductory chapter has offered something of an answer to the question, who are the civil servants? Now, we can attempt to understand what they do, how they are recruited and trained for these tasks, and weigh the importance of various reforms introduced in the realm of selection, particularly during the era of the new managerialism in the 1980s and 1990s.

Here, there and everywhere: the ubiquitous civil servant

In a key passage within the Ibbs Report, *Improving Management in Government: The next steps*, reference was made to the wide-ranging nature of the work carried out by civil servants: 'functions as diverse as driver licensing, fisheries protection, the catching of drug smugglers and the processing of Parliamentary Questions' (Efficiency Unit, 1988: para. 10). In fact, these functions might form the start of a seemingly endless catalogue of activities. It is impossible to construct an all-encompassing job profile for a 'typical' civil servant when we consider the fact that some people who work under this designation draft bills and help write ministerial speeches, while others are computer programmers, scientists, secretaries, telephonists, messengers, statisticians, librarians, economists, accountants and so on. Civil servants come into contact, directly or indirectly, with all of us, on a regular basis. They process our tax returns and provide us with appropriate tax codes, they compile and supply us with information about employment opportunities, they pay out unemployment and social security benefits as well as state pensions, they issue passports. Even when we have no contact with officials, their actions help to mould the society in which we live, as they advise governments on new policies and play a part in regulating the activities of many private-sector organisations. The ubiquitous civil servant seems to crop up just about everywhere!

Is it possible for us to bring some sort of order to the sprawling mass of jobs and activities sheltering under the huge umbrella labelled 'civil service'? Certainly, in the historical context, attempts have been made to establish broad demarcation lines. Northcote and Trevelyan, for example, established a fundamental functional division between 'mechanical' and 'intellectual' tasks, which had some meaning in an era when copying clerks and high policy advisers could be clearly differentiated and there was not a great deal of administrative activity between the two categories (Northcote and Trevelyan, 1854). Fulton was by no means the first to draw a descriptive distinction between 'generalists' and 'specialists', but his castigation of the 'cult of the generalist' firmly established the idea of an unacceptable division of talent and opportunity between the generalist administrators on the one hand, and the various experts, professionals and specialists on the other (Fulton, 1968). In recent years, it could be argued that there has been an increasing differentiation between those who might crudely be described as the Whitehall mandarins, the elite corps of officials working directly on a daily basis with ministers, and the varied ranks of managers charged with running the departments of state as efficient organisations and delivering services or implementing policy (increasingly through the medium of executive agencies). Beyond the mandarins and the managers, of course, are masses of civil servants who do not fit neatly into one or more all-encompassing categories. Official categorisations have tended to hinge on broad distinctions between 'industrial' and 'non-industrial' staff, and more detailed differentiation of occupational groups and grades. Table 2.1 provides the conventional breakdown of civil service occupational groups and grades.

Table 2.1   Civil service occupational groups and grades

Open Structure
Grade 1 (Permanent Secretary)
Grade 2 (Deputy Secretary)
Grade 3 (Under Secretary)
Grade 4
Grade 5
Grade 6
Grade 7

Administration Group
Senior Executive Officer
Higher Executive Officer (D)
Higher Executive Officer
Administration Trainee
Executive Officer
Administrative Officer
Administrative Assistant

Information Officer Group
Senior Information Officer
Information Officer
Assistant Information Officer

Statistician Group
Senior Assistant Statistician
Assistant Statistician

Science Group
Senior Scientific Officer
Higher Scientific Officer
Scientific Officer
Assistant Scientific Officer

Professional and Technology Group
Senior Professional and
  Technology Officer
Higher Professional and
  Technology Officer
Professional and Technology
  Officer
Professional and Technology
  Officer IV
Trainees
Technical Grade 1
Technical Grade 2

Economist Group
Senior Economic Assistant
Economic Assistant

Librarian Group
Senior Librarian
Librarian
Assistant Librarian

Social Security Group
Local Officer 1
Local Officer 2

Secretarial Group
Manager Grades
Senior Personal Secretary
Personal Secretary
Typist

Graphics Officer Group

Marine Services Group

Training Group

Legal Group

Curatorial Group

Police Group

Research Officer Group

The problem with rather neat descriptive or functional classifications is that, while they can be partially helpful in aiding comprehension at a general level, they can also mislead through over-simplification. Notwithstanding this limitation, in order to ease explanation, from time to time in the course of this book, reference will be made to what can be seen as three basic roles of the modern civil servant. The civil servant *qua* policy adviser is epitomised by the Whitehall mandarin. The civil servant *qua* departmental or agency manager will be primarily concerned with one or more of the various strands of financial, resource or personnel management. The civil servant *qua* policy or service executive, has day-to-day responsibility for directly or indirectly facilitating the detailed implementation of government policy and delivery of services to the public.

Let us now turn our attention to the themes and issues surrounding the recruitment and selection of these civil servants.

Recruitment and selection

'A staid organisation'?

The Northcote–Trevelyan Report of 1854 established the framework for a fundamental change in the nature of recruitment to the civil service. Although the Report's main recommendations were only introduced in a piecemeal fashion, before the end of the nineteenth century the old system of patronage, nepotism and jobbery had effectively been replaced by recruitment via competitive examination and promotion on merit (Pyper, 1991: 9–12). At the heart of the new system lay the Civil Service Commission, which was formed in 1855, answered to the monarch rather than the Prime Minister of the day (supposedly as a means of guaranteeing its independence from political patronage) and had its activities governed by Orders in Council as opposed to legislation. The Civil Service Order in Council of 1870 gave the Commission oversight of the competitive examination system.

Although there would be numerous technical changes to the methods of recruitment and selection over the years, and, of course, exceptional arrangements for placing 'outsiders' (businessmen, academics, scientists and others) in key posts during wartime

(Hennessy and Hague, 1985), the concept of entry to the service thereafter through competitive examination and promotion on merit remained largely unchallenged for over a century.

The route to the top of the career civil service lay via a steady progression through the grades of one of the 'classes' (although officials from the Administrative Class were at a considerable advantage in the promotion stakes). The structure was fairly rigid, none the less, and at its least flexible (for instance, in the 1930s), this tended to produce

> a staid organisation at virtually every level . . . a service in which the clerks were drawn from the secondary schools, the executive officers from the grammar school sixth forms and the administrators from the universities – careers for life with precious little movement from grade to grade . . . orthodoxy and hierarchy became entrenched.
> (Hennessy, 1989a: 87)

'Classes' were ultimately replaced by the more egalitarian-sounding 'groups'. A 'fast stream' was introduced, primarily to facilitate speedier promotion of university graduates who had been successful in their particular entrance examination and selection process (run by the Civil Service Selection Board, an offshoot of the Commission). These individuals were recruited into the Administrative Class (post-Fulton, Administration Trainees), and quickly introduced to life in the upper echelons of departments of state, with the expectation that they would be quickly promoted within the Open Structure of top grades. The Civil Service Commission retained fundamental control over the entire system of recruitment.

The Commission itself had enjoyed something of an arm's-length working relationship with the Treasury, its formal master, until it was transferred to the Civil Service Department in 1970. The demise of the CSD in 1981 saw the Commission relocated within the Management and Personnel Office (MPO), a part of the Cabinet Office. The MPO in its turn was transformed into the Office of the Minister for the Civil Service (a further reorganisation of the Cabinet Office in 1992 led to the creation of the Office of Public Service and Science, within which the Office of the Civil Service Commissioners was located. The Treasury retained ultimate control over recruitment policy in the sense that it made the key recommendations about the overall size of the civil service and the allocation of funds for recruitment purposes). The six Civil Service Commissioners (some of whom at any given time would be part-timers appointed from outside the civil service) and their small staff of officials were led by the First Commissioner.

Another offshoot of the Commission, the Senior Appointments Selection Committee, made recommendations to the Prime Minister for selection of civil servants to fill the most senior posts within the Open Structure (the top grades of the service, from Principal to Permanent Secretary, designated as open to applicants from all groupings as a result of a recommendation in the Fulton Report).

Such were the bare bones of the recruitment and selection system which had emerged, subject to occasional reform, by the 1970s. The system was criticised on a number of grounds, many of which were elucidated in the Fulton Report, and some of which continued to be heard in the years following Fulton, partly as a consequence either of the failure to implement Fulton's prescriptions for change or the flawed nature of the prescriptions themselves. The key criticisms were as follows:

- The closed entry system, within which senior civil service posts were exclusively open to those officials who had come up through the ranks, was said to have the effect of denying opportunities to talented and experienced 'outsiders' who might have a great deal to offer the service, and indeed the country, while insulating the civil servants themselves from potentially positive outside influences. This system has been characterised as the 'velvet drainpipe': a phrase attributed to the former Downing Street special adviser Bernard Donoughue, by Peter Hennessy (Hennessy, 1989a: 513).

- Top positions were filled predominantly by people moving up within the administrative grades, rather than from the ranks of the specialists or professionals (scientists, economists, statisticians and so on). The high-flying administrators were typically Oxbridge graduates with arts degrees. This 'cult of the generalist' was said by Fulton to be bad for the morale of those in the non-administrative grades and, more importantly, not in the long-term interests of a country facing the technological challenges of the late twentieth century.

- There was a perceived 'Oxbridge bias' in recruitment to the fast stream, with candidates from the Universities of Oxford and Cambridge performing disproportionately well in the entrance examinations and selection procedures. For example, candidates from these two universities provided 59 per cent of successful applicants to the fast stream in 1968.

- A lack of mobility characterised the lower ranks of the civil service in particular, with few opportunities for substantial promotion of those who had demonstrated considerable merit and ability following recruitment to the basic grades.

Not all of the criticisms were accepted by politicians, civil servants themselves or commentators. For example, the merits of the career civil service could be balanced against the weaknesses inherent in a closed entry system, the many-faceted requirements of work at the top level of the government machine might just suit the talents of the generalist administrator as opposed to the narrow specialist, and it could be argued (and was!) that the educational origins of successful applicants to the fast stream perhaps mattered less than securing the appointment of the best candidates. We shall return to the debates surrounding these issues at a later stage. In the meantime, however, we should note the changes to recruitment and selection methods which gathered pace from the 1980s.

Towards a more fluid, open system?

A series of developments starting in the 1980s brought about fairly important changes to certain aspects of the established systems of recruitment and selection. One general theme which is discernible from this period is a creeping decentralisation of recruitment and a concomitant weakening of the Civil Service Commission's grip. In order to understand the impact of these changes, it would make sense to look in turn at low- to middle-level appointments, the fast stream and senior appointments. As we proceed through these categories, consideration will be given to the alleged elitist and unrepresentative nature of fast-stream recruitment, and the potential threat posed to the concept of a career civil service by the expansion of 'lateral entry' systems.

Low- to middle-level appointments

The first signs of change in methods of recruitment could be discerned at the low and middle levels of the system. Under the 1982 Civil Service Order in Council, departments were given delegated power from 1983 to recruit directly to the junior grades, subject to selection on merit by fair and open competition. However, from the level of Executive Officer upwards (see Table 2.1 for a breakdown of the occupational groups and grades), the recruitment system remained fairly centralised, under the auspices of the Commission. The 1991 Civil Service Order in Council brought about a fundamental change in the status of the Commission, as we shall see, and transferred responsibility for recruitment to all grades below Grade 7 (the old Principal grade), with the sole exception of the fast-stream Administration Trainees, to departments and executive agencies. Departments and agencies had extended their area of responsibility over recruitment from 85 per cent a year post-1983 to over 95 per cent (Civil Service Commissioners, 1991: 3). By this stage, therefore, the role of the Civil Service Commission in the recruitment of officials from Administrative Assistants to Senior Executive Officers in the Administration Group (and the equivalent grades in the other occupational groups) was limited to ensuring that the rules laid down by the Minister for the Civil Service were being adhered to. The 1991 Order in Council, which is reproduced in full in the 1990–1 Civil Service Commissioners' Report (Civil Service Commissioners, 1991: Appendix D) placed the Commission under a new legal obligation to advise the Minister on the recruitment rules.

However, government departments and executive agencies now enjoyed considerable freedom of action in the realm of recruitment. They could operate their own recruitment schemes for the designated posts, or they could utilise the services of commercial agencies, as long as the Minister's rules were enforced in each case. Finally, they could turn to the newly created Recruitment and Assessment Services Agency. This Next Steps executive agency inherited the Civil Service Commission's recruitment functions in relation to posts below Grade 7, albeit on a new basis. The RAS was to have no 'tied' business, and it would therefore have to compete with commercial agencies for the right to deliver recruitment services to those government departments which did not choose to run their own recruitment schemes. A link between the Commission (now, technically, the Office of the Civil Service Commissioners) and the new RAS was secured through the appointment of the latter's Chief Executive as one of the Commissioners.

What are we to make of this change in the management of recruitment to the low and middle ranks of the civil service? While there would seem to be some positive advantages to be derived from a decentralised system, which is geared towards the achievement of value for money, and while it will be some time before a definitive judgement can be offered on the reform, it is only fair to recognise the potential risks associated with the new order:

> it may well be that the new arrangements, with departments and their regional offices doing their own advertising and recruitment, will be more expensive than the previous service provided by the specialist staff of the old Civil Service Commission. However, even if the new arrangements are cheaper, the modest extra expenditure incurred by the old Commission may turn out to have been worthwhile in terms of helping to guard against corruption and in terms of ensuring the practice of elements of democratic control. In other words, even if the new arrangements prove to be more economical . . . the old system may prove to have been more efficient. (Chapman, 1991: 3)

Fast stream

The responsibility of the Office of the Civil Service Commissioners for fast-stream recruitment remained unaffected by these new arrangements, although it decided to give the contract for this scheme to the RAS (Civil Service Commissioners, 1991: 3). It is something of a misnomer to speak of the fast stream: in fact there are several fast streams (for economists, statisticians, engineers and others, including European specialists), although the administration scheme, centred on entry to the Administration Trainee and Higher Executive Officer (Development) grades, tends to attract most attention, and this is the scheme to which we will mainly refer. It should be noted that a review of recruitment schemes conducted by the Treasury and the First Civil Service Commissioner in 1994 recommended abandoning the term 'fast stream', on the grounds that it confuses recruitment *per se* with the later process of identifying people with top management potential. The

government indicated that this proposal would be given serious consideration (Prime Minister, 1994: 39).

Controversy surrounding the 'Oxbridge bias', which is said to characterise entry to the fast stream, has already been mentioned, and this critique is often broadened to encompass negative analyses of fast-stream recruitment with reference to the under-representation of women and ethnic minorities. Before looking at these matters in slightly more detail, the basic mechanisms of recruitment at this level should be understood.

Applicants for the fast stream may be in-service candidates (who are mainly Executive Officers), final-year Honours students or graduates holding first- or second-class Honours degrees. The first stage of the process is the sifting of candidates through centralised marking of the application form. Stage 2, the Qualifying Test, involves a series of six aptitude tests, focused on comprehension, composition, drafting, statistical, numeracy and general intelligence exercises. These are taken over a full day at regional centres. A very high proportion of applicants are rejected at these early stages. For example, out of 9,938 applicants in 1992, only 784, or 7.9 per cent, survived the sifting process and the Qualifying Test. The third stage takes place at the Civil Service Selection Board (CSSB, or 'Cizbee') in London, and involves a two-day examination (via simulated tasks, cognitive tests and one-to-one interviews) of small groups of candidates by teams of assessors (usually three, including a serving Grade 7 civil servant, a senior or recently retired member of the public service and a psychologist). The CSSB recommends candidates to the Final Selection Board (FSB, or 'Fizbee'), where intensive interviews are conducted by a Civil Service Commissioner, two senior civil servants and two outsiders (an academic and an industrialist, for example). In 1992, 139 candidates were recommended for appointment following the deliberations of the FSB, representing 1.4 per cent of the original applicants (29 out of 96, or 30.2 per cent, of in-service candidates were successful).

Is the 'Oxbridge bias' still apparent? What can be said about recruitment to the fast stream of women and candidates from the ethnic minorities? The Civil Service Commissioners, and indeed, the Head of the Civil Service, have shown a sensitivity towards the matter of the so-called 'Oxbridge bias' in recruitment to the fast stream, to the extent that they are quick to respond in print to newspaper articles which mention this phenomenon. The facts show that applicants from the Universities of Oxford and Cambridge still perform disproportionately well in the fast-stream competition, although the Oxbridge successes are not quite as marked as they have been in the past. It has already been pointed out that in 1968, the year of Fulton, Oxbridge provided 59 per cent of the successful candidates. In 1982, the figure was a spectacular 71 per cent. For the three competitions between 1990 and 1992, the Oxbridge success rates were 46, 48 and 48 per cent respectively (Civil Service Commissioners, 1991; 1992; 1993).

It cannot be denied that steps have been taken over the years to address the Oxbridge issue. The Civil Service Commissioners are duty-bound to appoint the best candidates, regardless of their social or educational origins, and, of course, the success of Oxbridge candidates for entry to the upper echelons of the civil service is no more than a mirror of the success of such candidates in competition for entry to the professions and other prized careers. In this sense, the civil service figures could be seen as either a reflection of the inherent superiority of Oxbridge graduates, or an indication of wider social phenomena.

Alternatively, we might conclude that a real bias, conscious or otherwise, is at work. If the evidence is examined closely, it is all but impossible to detect a conscious bias in favour of candidates from Oxford and Cambridge. The Qualifying Tests are marked 'blind', in the sense that the names and institutions of the candidates are unknown to the examiners, while steps have been taken in recent years to open up the CSSB and FSB procedures to new, outside influences. If bias is operating, it must be of the unconscious sort, whereby an institution unwittingly recruits its potential high-flyers of the future in the image of the dominant group of current and past senior figures. Bias of this kind is extremely difficult to detect, let alone remedy. Furthermore, one can point to a range of positive measures undertaken by the Civil Service Commission in order to reduce further the risk of excluding potential applicants from outside the traditional strong recruiting grounds.

The Office of the Civil Service Commissioners' Graduate and Schools Liaison Section annually organises a series of conferences for school and university careers advisers, in addition to the 'Graduates in Government' careers information fairs, and scores of visits to schools and institutions of higher education. Beyond these activities, in 1991 Sir Robin Butler, the Head of the Civil Service, launched an initiative with the specific intention of widening the recruitment net for the fast stream. Whitehall Permanent Secretaries and agency Chief Executives were asked to 'adopt' a university (or, at that stage, a polytechnic), for the purpose of visiting in order to encourage students to consider applying for the fast stream. It was perhaps an intended irony that Sir Robin, a product of Harrow and University College Oxford adopted Thames Polytechnic, while the only mandarin who had left school at 16 without proceeding to higher education, Sir Peter Kemp, adopted Oxford University! Less happily for this strategy, however, the effective dismissal of Peter Kemp from the civil service in the summer of 1992 was cited, not least by Kemp himself, as evidence of the continued dominance of the Oxbridge ethos at the top levels of the service (Brown, 1992).

When we turn our attention to ethnic trends in fast-stream recruitment, we face a problem. It is difficult to provide accurate figures with respect to the recruitment of people of ethnic minority origin, for two reasons. First, the figures published by the Civil Service Commission only show the ethnic origin of external applicants for the fast stream: the details of in-service candidates are not provided. Secondly, a proportion of candidates fail to respond to the ethnic questionnaire. Bearing these limitations in mind, we can say that by the 1990s 6–8 per cent of applicants for the fast stream were classified as being of ethnic origin, with 0–2 per cent of the posts being filled by non-whites (Civil Service Commissioners, 1991; 1992; 1993). In successive reports during the 1990s, the Commissioners addressed this issue in terms which indicated a growing concern. Whereas in 1991 they were content to note that efforts were being made to 'promote awareness of civil service careers amongst the ethnic minority population' (Civil Service Commissioners, 1991: 9), by the following year it was accepted that the reasons for the low success rates of ethnic minority candidates required 'further examination' (Civil Service Commissioners, 1992: 6). The 1993 Report devoted a full page to the matter of low success rates among ethnic minorities (Civil Service Commissioners, 1993: 8). It was noted that the numbers of ethnic minority applicants had increased significantly over recent years, but this was not yet reflected in successes. Beyond improving the information available to candidates about the selection process in general, and the Qualifying Test in particular (the hurdle at which the highest proportion of candidates fall), there was no clear indication of future strategy in respect of this issue.

By the 1990s, in general terms, women tended to account for around 40 per cent of the total applicants for the fast stream, and approximately 33 per cent of those appointed in any given year (Civil Service Commissioners, 1991; 1992; 1993). Once again, albeit to a less marked degree than is true for the non-Oxbridge, non-white elements of the potential recruitment pool, the figures suggest a disproportionately poor success rate.

Senior appointments

Methods of recruitment and selection for the top seven grades of the civil service changed remarkably within a relatively short period of time in the late 1980s and early 1990s. The old closed entry system for the top posts was effectively replaced by a system which bore many (although not all) of the characteristics of the 'lateral entry model' (Hood, 1991). Under the latter, senior positions are effectively open to all-comers. The potential consequences of this for the concept of a career civil service will be discussed in due course, but for the time being, let us examine the causes and the nature of the changes.

The 'velvet drainpipe' syndrome, referred to above, epitomised a critical view of the civil service, variants of which could be found in Fulton's attack on the 'amateur' nature of the service, right-wing distrust of overweening bureaucrats content to build their own empires, and left-wing suspicion of 'establishment' mandarins wedded to the *status quo*. Margaret Thatcher's approach to this involved manipulating the existing system by adopting a markedly pro-active attitude towards the work of the Senior Appointments Selection Committee, to the point where the names of her favoured candidates for promotion were more or less openly touted before the Committee. This led to the accusation that promotion at the top levels of the service was more likely to be gained if you were 'one of us'. The controversy surrounding this matter is discussed in Chapter 4.

The idea of opening up the service to new blood, perhaps through explicit politicisation, perhaps in other less dramatic ways, had been around for some time, when, in 1986, the Treasury and

Civil Service Select Committee of the House of Commons came out in favour of a limited opening up of senior posts to outsiders, under the supervision of the Civil Service Commission. 'We believe that there should be regular infusions, temporary and permanent, of highly motivated people of proven ability into the higher Civil Service' (Treasury and Civil Service Committee, 1986: para. 5.18). The Royal Institute of Public Administration added its weight to the argument:

> only about two per cent of the members of the Senior Open Structure are 'outsiders' temporarily brought in to fill particular vacancies. Whitehall is too cautious in this respect. More could be done centrally to liaise with business, universities and the rest of the public sector to seek out talent. More civil service posts should be publicly advertised, and applications for them encouraged from the existing civil service and from outside Whitehall. (RIPA, 1987: 61)

Three developments, the so-called Levene affair, the Next Steps initiative and the changing role of the Civil Service Commissioners, were markers on the path to reform.

By the late 1970s it had become established that people could be appointed to senior posts in the civil service from the private sector or other 'outside' spheres, provided no internal candidate could offer the required knowledge, experience or expertise. It has been estimated that approximately seventy top posts were filled in this way between 1979 and 1985 (Drewry and Butcher, 1991: 103). It took the Levene affair in 1984 to draw attention to this trend, and bring about some clarification of the rules surrounding the appointment of outsiders.

Peter Levene, special political adviser to the Defence Secretary, Michael Heseltine, had been Chairman of United Scientific Holdings, a defence contracting company. When Heseltine appointed Levene as Chairman of Defence Procurement for the MoD, at a salary of £95,000 (twice the going rate for the job), while formally on secondment from his firm, without consulting the Civil Service Commission, a political row ensued. The Commission, together with the House of Commons Defence Select Committee and the Public Accounts Committee, sought clarification of the procedure to be followed when making such appointments. What emerged, in 1986, was a dispensation to departments to make appointments for up to five years below Grade 3 (Under Secretary), provided Civil

Service Commission guidelines regarding the appointment of the best-qualified candidates were adhered to. In the case of fixed-term appointments at and above Grade 3, and all fixed-term appointments of more than five years, the Commission would participate directly in the recruitment process.

This delegation of power from the Commission preceded, but was very much within the spirit of, the 1991 Civil Service Order in Council. After 1991, departments and agencies continued to be free to conduct their own recruitment for fixed-term sub-Grade 3 appointments, in line with the 1986 dispensation, or, alternatively they could utilise the services of the RAS or a commercial agency. By this stage, approximately 150 fixed-term appointments (including inward secondments) were being made each year at Grades 3–7 (Civil Service Commissioners, 1992: 20–1; 1993: 22–3).

Fixed-term appointments were one manifestation of a new fluidity at the top levels of the civil service, but the trend did not stop there. National advertising of vacancies and open competitions for posts, in line with the 'lateral entry model', became more common from the late 1980s. To a large extent, the Next Steps initiative provided a testing ground for this process, although the government's announcement of a whole series of 'pay and management flexibilities' in 1989 served to fill in some of the details.

Following the launch of Next Steps in 1988, the government made it clear that selection of Chief Executives for the new executive agencies was to be a matter for Secretaries of State in the parent departments. The basic aim was to ensure that the best-qualified person was appointed as Chief Executive for each agency, regardless of whether the person came from within or outside the civil service. Ministers could appoint from within the civil service without a formal competition, or, alternatively, appoint a civil service or an external candidate by means of an open competition following public advertisement of the post. Open competitions were strongly favoured by the Treasury and Civil Service Select Committee in successive reports:

> Open competition should prove to be an effective way of unearthing talent inside as well as outside the Service, and therefore we repeat the recommendation made in our last Report on Next Steps that open competitions should be held for the appointment of all agency Chief Executives. Furthermore, as the decision whether or not to hold an open competition is ultimately a ministerial one, we recommend that

the Minister should give an explanation of every case in which it is decided not to hold an open competition for the appointment of a Chief Executive. (Treasury and Civil Service Committee, 1990a: para. 28)

While the government was not prepared to compel ministers to explain their appointment procedures in this fashion, it was clear that there existed a bias towards open competition for these posts. By the summer of 1994, 100 Chief Executives and Chief Executive designate appointments had been made. Of these, 69 were the result of open competitions, which produced 37 successes by non-civil-service candidates (Next Steps Team, 1994: para. 21). Thus, 37 per cent of all Chief Executives were appointed from outside the civil service.

This trend was important in its own right, and also because it was indicative of a wider development within the civil service. By 1993, more than half of all civil servants were working in executive agencies run by Chief Executives, a substantial majority of whom had been appointed following national advertisement of, and open competition for, their posts. Furthermore, even beyond the executive agencies, 'Next Steps practices' were spreading, to the extent that large numbers of senior posts were being filled through open competition. Gone were the days when access to the top grades of the civil service lay almost exclusively via the 'velvet drainpipe'. Excluding the agency Chief Executives, between 1991 and 1993 eighteen appointees to posts in Grades 1–3 (the senior Open Structure), and 859 appointees to posts in Grades 4–7, came from outside the civil service (Civil Service Commissioners, 1993: 4). The role of the Commissioners in such appointments was to give prior written approval for the posts to be filled by outsiders, and, thereafter, to participate in the selection procedure:

> We have worked closely with departments and agencies to ensure that recruitment work has been carried out efficiently and effectively within agreed arrangements to support selection on merit through fair and open competition. For most competitions at Grades 1 to 3 level, the First Civil Service Commissioner has participated directly in the key stages of the selection process. At Grades 4 to 7 level, we nominate the chairman, usually through Recruitment and Assessment Services (RAS), who have also acted on our behalf at key stages of recruitment. (Civil Service Commissioners, 1993: 5)

This represented something of a change from the past monopoly of the Civil Service Commission over senior appointments. Further, incremental change was proposed in 1994, when the very concept of senior posts was revised.

The government announced its intention to restructure the top ranks of the civil service, in order to produce 'leaner, flatter management structures with less emphasis on working through hierarchies and more scope for talented individuals to make their mark' (Prime Minister, 1994: 35). Whereas the existing senior Open Structure covered Grades 1–3, the new Senior Civil Service, to be created by 1996, would encompass staff at Grade 5 and above as well as all agency Chief Executives. While the bulk of posts at this level would continue to be filled by internal appointment, the option of competition (service-wide, or full open competition) would be considered by departments filling all vacancies within the Senior Civil Service. The respective roles of departments, the Civil Service Commissioners and the Senior Appointments Selection Committee in relation to posts within the old senior Open Structure, would remain intact in relation to posts within the new Senior Civil Service. Explicit, written contracts (which might be fixed-term in some cases) would be given to officials in these senior posts.

While entry to the top ranks of the British civil service was far removed from the type of politicised 'spoils' system to be found in the United States, for example (see the discussion in the introductory chapter of the characteristics of Britain's 'permanent, neutral' system compared with the alternatives), the trend towards open competition for senior posts signified something of a break with tradition. Appointment on merit, within rules established by the Minister for the Civil Service and monitored by the Civil Service Commissioners, remained the order of the day. However, the old closed entry system, Bernard Donoughue's 'velvet drainpipe', was no longer intact. Perhaps something of a happy medium was evolving, in traditional British constitutional fashion. Certainly not a politicised 'spoils' system, nor an unrestricted lateral entry system, but no longer a traditional closed entry system either. Something between the latter two, a modified lateral entry system. Could this achieve the best of both worlds?

The risks associated with discarding the career civil service were stressed in the early 1980s as a number of retired mandarins attempted to rebut the arguments of Sir John Hoskyns (a former Downing Street special adviser) in favour of overt politicisation (Pyper, 1984: 380–3). The key points deserve repetition, not because the new trends in recruitment to the top grades represent an end to the career civil service as yet (although some commentators have written in fairly apocalyptic terms to this effect – see, for example, O'Toole, 1993), but because there is a need for a balance to be maintained between the obvious benefits which accrue from the influx of new talent and the potential disadvantages of taking the lateral entry model too far.

First, reserving the most senior posts exclusively or mainly for outsiders recruited under the existing rules (let alone political appointees), runs the risk of sacrificing what a former Head of the Civil Service called 'collective and historical knowledge' in the departments of state (Wass, 1983). In other words, the experience built up over decades within departments, and the common culture which emerges in organisations where there are key elements of continuity, could be needlessly discarded.

Secondly, if the top posts are seen to be the preserve of talented outsiders, to the exclusion of the officials seeking promotion from more junior ranks, this could have a disastrous impact on morale, as well as seriously inhibiting the recruitment of talented and ambitious people to the lower grades.

Thirdly, unless the rules on recruitment and appointment are continuously and rigorously enforced (and this might become more difficult if lateral entry were to become the norm across the full range of senior posts), there is the risk of what we might describe as 'Caligula's horse' syndrome. It will be recalled that the Roman Emperor Gaius Caligula was said to have tried to appoint his horse as Consul. Unnatural appointments to the senior grades of the British civil service may not be likely, even under an unrestrained lateral entry system, but unethical ones cannot be discounted.

The recruitment and selection of civil servants has undergone fairly substantial change over recent years. The new arrangements are characterised by increased flexibility and decentralisation, and they are at one with the federalisation of the civil service. Departments and agencies have come to enjoy an unprecedented opportunity to choose their own methods of recruitment for nearly all grades below Grade 7. At the top levels, the traditional closed entry system is being superseded by what we have termed a modified lateral entry system. It is likely to take some time for the effects of the changes to become clear, but a return to the old regime of recruitment and selection would seem unlikely.

Having examined the main issues surrounding the recruitment and selection of civil servants, our next task is to enquire into the training they receive once in post.

Training and development

Sitting next to Nellie

As Drewry and Butcher have observed:

> Perhaps the most prominent feature of the British tradition of civil service training is that there is not very much of it, at least in any formal sense . . . the traditional view of civil service training as being the icing on the cake of experience remains the dominant one. (Drewry and Butcher, 1991: 110–11)

The British civil service remained a bastion of what can variously be described as 'sitting next to Nellie', 'learning by doing' or 'on-the-job training' long after these approaches had been dismissed as inadequate in comparable administrative machines abroad. Even when the value and significance of training had been accorded some recognition in Whitehall and beyond, this was done in a rather half-hearted fashion. Centralised training provision was to remain limited, with considerable scope for discretion given to individual departments and agencies. A guide to life in the civil service, published by the First Division Association in 1990, noted wide variations in the use of training courses by departments, and commented on the gulf between the theoretical entitlement of 15–20 training days per year for fast-stream entrants, and the reality of line managers being reluctant to release officials from the demands of daily work (First Division Association, 1990: 23–4).

While devolved responsibility for elements of training and staff development is necessary, critics of the British approach argue that devolution can be confused with diffusion, so that overall control of, and responsibility for, key aspects of training may be lost.

Even allowing for the considerable political, historical, social and constitutional differences between the two states, a sharp comparison is often drawn between the provision for training of civil servants in France and in Britain. Technical and specialist civil servants in France undergo rigorous training at the Ecole Polytechnique, while those who are being groomed for the highest administrative posts are trained in the Ecole Nationale d'Administration (ENA). The ENA, which was established in 1945, is an elitist forcing ground for the senior officials. It combines many of the characteristics of a prestigious university and a staff college. In Britain, the opportunity to argue the case for a training institution of this calibre was perhaps lost in 1944, when a committee chaired by the Financial Secretary to the Treasury, Ralph Assheton, recognised the need for a move away from the creed of learning by doing, but only felt able to recommend the introduction of a short course for the graduate entrant Assistant Principals.

This three-week 'Junior Administration Course' was duly set up under the auspices of a new Training and Education Division within the Treasury, in 1945 (Bird, 1992: 71). Eighteen years later an attempt was made to give training a slightly higher profile through the establishment of the Treasury's Centre for Administrative Studies (CAS), which ran introductory courses for direct-entry Principals as well as the graduate entrants. Thus, only a very small proportion of the civil service had access to what might be described as proper training, and this was of an exclusively introductory type.

For most civil servants, training was limited at best, and provided to suit the convenience of the trainers as opposed to the trainees. This can be illustrated with reference to the experience of a man who joined the Home Office as a direct-entry Principal in 1968. He was immediately placed at the head of a small division responsible for setting up the government's new Urban Aid Programme, which had an annual budget of £12 million:

> I had an induction course of just three days, which consisted mainly of visiting other new entrants who had joined in mid-career. . . . All this was most interesting, but not much help in tackling the intricacies of legislation or the Rate Support Grant. And I needed help, for within a few weeks . . . I was sitting in the official box in the House of Commons passing notes to our Minister, Merlyn Rees, on the Second Reading of the Bill to set up the Urban Programme. (Bird, 1992: 72–3)

This official was sent on a three-week 'Introduction to Government' course which included detailed guidance on steering a Bill through Parliament: unfortunately this was two months after the Urban Programme Bill had received Royal Assent!

The Fulton Committee's wide-ranging investigation of the civil service covered, *inter alia*, the issue of training. In retrospect, it could be argued that another great opportunity was lost at this stage, but that verdict might be rather unfair: perhaps the real flaw was in the implementation of Fulton's proposals. Whatever one's view, Fulton fell far short of propounding the need for a British version of the ENA. The Fulton Report, published in 1968, recommended the establishment of a new Civil Service College charged with the provision of major training courses in administration and management (for graduate entrants, specialists and those moving into senior positions), shorter courses in both management and vocational subjects (for more junior officials) and with conducting research into administrative issues (this research function was never activated).

Civil Service College: not the ENA

The Civil Service College was set up in 1970. Initially, it was headed by a Deputy Secretary (Grade 2), and based at three centres, London, Sunningdale in Berkshire and Edinburgh. However, before too long the declining status of the College became apparent, and even the potential threat of a more centralised training regime was dissipated. Within a period of a few months in 1976–7, the post of College Principal was downgraded to Under Secretary (Grade 3), and the Edinburgh centre was closed on economic grounds.

In organisational terms, the Civil Service College was linked, in turn, to the Treasury, the Civil Service Department and various offshoots of the Cabinet Office, culminating in the Office of Public Service and Science, from 1992. By that stage, indeed, from 1989, the College had assumed a new status as a Next Steps executive agency.

Three general comments should be made about the role of the Civil Service College in training and staff development. First, the College was never a staff college or an elitist forcing ground on ENA lines. Officials were not, and are not, required to attend and pass College courses before qualifying for promotion to and within the senior ranks of the civil service, although in certain circumstances it may be advantageous for them to have done so. However, as we shall see, there is a sense in which the College is more elitist than heretofore, since by far the highest proportion of the officials attending the College now come from the top grades of the civil service.

Secondly, the College offers a wide range of courses, designed for officials at various stages of their careers. In addition to what might be described as the 'flagship' training modules designed for the fast-stream entrants, courses are offered, for example, in the fields of management studies, statistics and operational research, information technology and management services, as well as a range of externally validated qualifications. Additionally, the College played a significant role in disseminating information about the successive waves of structural and managerial change which engulfed the civil service during the 1980s and 1990s. Thus, officials having to cope with the broad thrust and detailed implications of the Rayner scrutinies, the Financial Management Initiative, Next Steps and market testing, would be served by lectures, seminars, day and residential courses run by the College. During 1992–3, a total of 15,141 students attended the Civil Service College (Chancellor of the Duchy of Lancaster, 1993: 30). This represented a substantial fall in numbers from the mid-1980s, when around 26,000 students would attend the College each year. Nearly 52 per cent of the students attending the College in 1992–3 were from Grade 7 and above (the Open Structure): a marked change from the mid-1980s, when only around 18 per cent of the students came from these grades (Drewry and Butcher, 1991: 113).

Thirdly, the College does not enjoy a monopoly in the sphere of civil service training. In the early 1980s the free provision of College courses to government departments ceased, and a charging regime was introduced. Subsequently, departments and agencies were allowed to choose between sending their officials to the College for training courses, providing courses 'in-house' or utilising commercial training agencies. On becoming an executive agency in 1989, the Civil Service College was required to cover its costs from income, as well as meeting a number of performance criteria (Civil Service College, 1989), including a specific value-for-money target and securing a number of private-sector students each year (the latter has remained small: 700, or under 5 per cent of all students, attended the College in 1992–3). Thus, the Civil Service College is only one provider of training, competing for business with many others.

The implications of this are important, and bring us back to one of the themes mentioned at the outset of this section. There is a marked, and increasing, diffusion of responsibility for training within the civil service. This tendency is perhaps not unrelated to the broader theme of decentralisation epitomised by the Next Steps initiative. In other words, in training, as in other spheres, we seem to be witnessing a move towards what might be described as a more federal, less unitary structure, although, as we have pointed out, decentralisation, devolution and diffusion have ever been the watchwords of civil service training. This topic of service-wide organisational change is a matter for discussion at a later stage in the book. For the time being, with particular reference to the current theme, we can note that some departments and agencies now offer an extremely wide range of training courses 'in-house', or in conjunction with commercial training agencies. This can be illustrated with reference to one department, the Scottish Office.

During 1992–3 the Personnel Division of the Scottish Office offered 207 training courses to staff, ranging from half-day modules to five-day residential blocks (Scottish Office, 1992). One-third more training was being carried out in-house compared with 1989. Most grades were receiving something in excess of the Scottish Office's target of three days' training per year, although very few of the courses were compulsory. The courses themselves ranged from very general staff development modules on topics such as 'Assertiveness' and 'Creative Thinking' to those designed to meet the specific needs of purchasing and finance managers, and others geared to the requirements of people working in close proximity to ministers (the 'Ministerial Modules'). Within the latter, courses covered topics including 'Appearing before a Select Committee', 'Bill Work', 'Parliamentary Questions', 'Ministerial Correspondence' and 'Speech Writing'. Only a handful of courses were specifically tailored for fast-stream entrants, Grade 7 staff or above, but all staff were reminded that support and funding would not be given for attendance at Civil Service College courses where an in-house equivalent existed (Scottish Office, 1992: 47).

Praiseworthy though this type of provision may be, it should be noted that there are wide discrepancies in the levels of formal training offered by different departments and agencies (Plowden, 1994: 27–8). The general level of training on offer within the civil service remains open to the criticism that it

> is not enough to enable a major organisation to maintain a steady state in a turbulent environment. It is not nearly enough if there is a serious intention to change organisational values, or to establish and maintain a coherent set of values in the face of increasing inward or outward mobility. (Plowden, 1994: 31)

At the outset of its extensive examination of the state of the civil service, the Treasury and Civil Service Committee of the House of Commons identified career development and training as a major area of concern and took evidence on this key issue (Treasury and Civil Service Committee, 1993).

We have set out the mechanisms and procedures through which people are recruited into the civil service, and selected for promotion once in post. The increasing, albeit belated and patchy, emphasis given to training and development has been examined. If this particular 'Cinderella' has not yet gone to the ball, at least there are some signs that her fairy godmother may be about to bestow more suitable clothes upon her! Now, we set our sights on the civil service as an organisation.

3

CHANGING SIZE, SHAPE AND CULTURE

In order to make sense of the civil service as an organisation (or, perhaps more accurately now, as a federation of organisations), we must examine its scale and structure, as well as the attempts which have been made to change its form and organisational culture. To begin with, let us address the issue of numbers, which became highly politicised in the context of the Conservative Governments' attempts to cut the public sector down to size.

The numbers game and the nature of bureaucracy

For most of the twentieth century, the civil service grew steadily, as the machinery of government responded to the demands placed upon it by welfare reforms and the imperatives of war. A reasonably clear picture emerges from a review of the official statistics, although it is impossible to be precise due to inconsistencies in the methods of calculation, particularly in the period before 1945. The figures which follow represent totals for the industrial and non-industrial civil service (Drewry and Butcher, 1991: 48; HM Treasury, 1993: 46). They are presented graphically in Figure 3.1.

In 1901 there were around 116,000 civil servants. By the eve of the First World War, this figure had risen to over 282,000, as government assumed new regulatory and service functions in the realms of industry and social policy. The civil service expanded

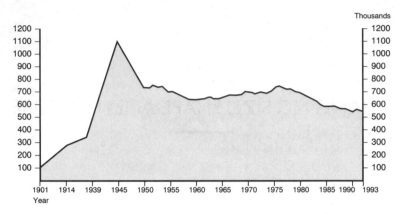

Figure 3.1   Size of the civil service

with an influx of temporary 'outsiders' during the war, and then, following peacetime contraction, settled down to a period of gradual expansion again in the inter-war period. By 1939, the service was 347,000 strong. Once again, war necessitated rapid expansion, to the extent that there were 1,114,000 civil servants by 1945.

The challenge of managing the post-war welfare state saw the service stabilise at well over 700,000 in the early 1950s. Thereafter, industrial civil servants formed a declining proportion of the total due to the discontinuation or privatisation of many functions performed by this group. By 1992, over 89 per cent of civil servants would be categorised as non-industrial, with the great majority of 'industrials' working as firemen, electricians, carpenters, fitters, cleaners and messengers, in the Ministry of Defence.

Margaret Thatcher's Government inherited what she saw as a bloated and inefficient bureaucracy of 732,000 officials in 1979, and immediately launched a twin-pronged attack on numbers and methods of work. Although the Conservatives succeeded in getting the numbers down by almost a quarter, to under 554,000 by 1991, the total rose again to 565,319 (over 504,000 of whom were non-industrial) the following year, and elements of the Conservative press expressed fears about a lost opportunity to cut even deeper (HM Treasury, 1992a; Hadfield and Reeve, 1993). The total fell again to 554,000 in 1993, and a further cut, to 533,000, was

Figure 3.2   On the news that the government wished to see civil service numbers fall below 500,000. (Source: *The Times*, 14 July 1994)

achieved by the spring of 1994 (HM Treasury, 1993; Prime Minister, 1994), at which point the government announced its desire to see numbers fall 'significantly below 500,000' (see Figure 3.2).

Perhaps it is significant that the words 'bloated' and 'inefficient' were juxtaposed with 'bureaucracy' above. The concept of bureaucracy is complex and sophisticated, but, in the context of the British civil service (and most other organisations in both the private and the public sectors), it is now almost invariably used in a negative sense.

This is rather unfortunate, and somewhat confusing, since the theories of bureaucracy developed at the turn of the century by the German sociologist Max Weber, and refined by countless academics thereafter, are essentially neutral. Indeed, Weber's bureaucratic system is but the purest form of what he described as 'rational–legal rule', a form of government within which authority and power are given a formal legal base, and an administrative staff provide the means by which those with lawful political power can govern (Page, 1992: 7–8). In this sense, a bureaucracy can be viewed as a vital component of a democratic state. It is not intrinsically associated with red tape, the dominance of officials over elected politicians, secrecy, obstructionism and petty empire-building. Furthermore, in its ideal form, a bureaucracy places great emphasis on technical expertise and discipline and efficiency.

Thus we do not need to use the term 'bureaucratic' in an unreflective, negative fashion. Instead, we should perhaps be prepared to examine the flaws and inefficiencies of bureaucracy in much the same spirit as we do those of democracy: not in the search for some fundamentally different system, but in the pursuit of progressive improvement.

Structural and organisational change: an overview

One way of understanding the changes which have taken place in the size, organisational shape and culture of the British civil service over recent times is to think in terms of two inter-related types of change. The first we could term 'micro' change: meaning the advent of new administrative and managerial techniques, practices and procedures, often of a very detailed nature. The second, 'macro' change, refers to overall structural reform, adjustments to the geography of the civil service. Before considering the specific characteristics and impact of these two types of change, it is important for us to chart their contemporary development and locate them within a reasonably broad perspective. First, however, it would be appropriate to make some comments about the allocation of responsibility for the overall running of the civil service.

Who manages civil service change?

Formal responsibility for the central, strategic management of the civil service resides with the occupant of 10 Downing Street, who is Minister for the Civil Service as well as being Prime Minister and First Lord of the Treasury. Traditionally, Prime Ministers found it convenient to channel this aspect of their power through the Treasury. Treasury control over the civil service was strengthened considerably during a period of a few months in 1919 and 1920 (Pyper, 1991: 16–17), and was never fully relinquished. Sir Warren Fisher, Head of the Civil Service between 1919 and 1939, was simultaneously Permanent Secretary to the Treasury. Thereafter, it became more common for the headship of the Civil Service to fall upon the Cabinet Secretary, although there have been periods when the post has been held jointly by the Cabinet Secretary and the Permanent Secretary to the Treasury.

Between 1968 and 1981 the Civil Service Department was nominally charged with the central management function, but the Treasury ultimately succeeded in steadily and stealthily reclaiming its authority over key aspects of service-wide management. The dismantling of the CSD in 1981 (see Chapter 1) saw the emergence of a new Treasury – Cabinet Office – 10 Downing Street axis, which was to dominate the management of the civil service thereafter.

Following the 1992 General Election, elements of the Cabinet Office were restructured, and a new Office of Public Service and Science (OPSS) was established, within which were units charged with, *inter alia*, responsibility for the Next Steps programme, the Citizen's Charter, civil service efficiency, recruitment and appointments. The Treasury's overall control over the pay and grading systems remained intact.

The Prime Minister aside, there are four key individuals in the general management of the civil service as a whole. On the ministerial side, the Chancellor of the Duchy of Lancaster (David Hunt) heads the OPSS, while, on the official side, the Cabinet Secretary and Head of the Civil Service (Sir Robin Butler) is the single most important figure, although the Permanent Secretary to the Treasury (Sir Terry Burns) and the Permanent Secretary of the Office of Public Service and Science (Richard Mottram) have important parts to play.

Managerialism, giantism and hiving-off, c. 1961–79

To some extent, it can be argued that modest organisational change has been a recurring theme in the modern history of the civil service. However, the pace and nature of change (of both the micro and macro variety) has intensified over recent years. We can trace back to the 1960s and 1970s most of the themes of structural and managerial reform which would come to dominate the service in the last two decades of the century.

As elements of the surface complacency of British government came to be punctured by growing evidence of relative economic decline (or, at best, stagnation), so attention began to focus on aspects of the system which seemed to be in need of modernisation. The civil service did not escape scrutiny.

While the techniques and processes of management in government had attracted passing interest from ministers and senior civil servants in the past, the Plowden Report of 1961 signalled the beginnings of a new managerialist agenda. Primarily concerned with developing new systems to aid in controlling public expenditure, Plowden also roamed over the broad territory of managerial reform. Although the report did not prescribe specific reforms in this sphere, it did stress the increasing importance of financial management at all levels of the administrative hierarchy, and the need to breed a new generation of civil service managers who would be *au fait* with modern management theory and practice.

Fulton returned to this theme, in considerably more detail. Over the next few years, a range of Fulton-inspired reforms were introduced, with the general aim of transforming the management of the civil service. Management services units were set up within departments, and the principles of 'management by objectives' and accountable management, were stressed.

However, the first serious attempt to co-ordinate micro and macro change, to combine a concern with the detail of managerial reform within the departments of state with an overall plan for restructuring the government machine, was put in place by the Conservative Government of Edward Heath after 1970.

In opposition, Heath and his advisers (some of whom were businessmen keen to see the most recent managerial practices transplanted from the private to the public sector) had planned a 'Quiet Revolution' which would modernise the systems and processes of British government. In the wake of the 1970 election victory, a small team of businessmen, headed by Richard Meyjes from Shell, and including Derek Rayner from Marks and Spencer, came into Whitehall on extended sabbaticals from their firms. Within four months, the defining document of the 'Quiet Revolution' was published. The October 1970 White Paper, *The Reorganisation of Central Government* (White Paper, 1970), identified reform of the machinery of government as a major priority of the government.

In retrospect, three themes can be discerned in the period that followed: the creation of a smaller number of large departments of state (this came to be known as 'giantism'), a limited experiment with 'hiving-off' some departmental functions into new agencies (as recommended by Fulton, and supported by the 1970 White Paper), and the propagation of new techniques and procedures for management and policy analysis.

The Heath Government picked up the idea of creating super-departments, partly as a means of enhancing management of the civil service, from the current 'big is beautiful' vogue in the private sector, and from the Wilson Government's initiatives in this direction (the creation of the Department of Health and Social Security (DHSS) in 1968 was the prime example of Wilsonian giantism). Giantism was to accommodate a more rational allocation of departments to policy spheres, while achieving substantial economies of scale. Such was the theory. In practice, the new super-departments, including the Department of the Environment, the DHSS, and the Department of Trade and Industry, brought their own problems. Heath and his successors discovered that political considerations (such as the need to find suitably weighty posts for Cabinet colleagues), new policy priorities and the unwieldy nature of the giants forced something of a retreat from the pure form of giantism promulgated by the 1970 White Paper.

Even before the end of the Heath Government, the DTI was breaking up, with a new Department of Energy floating away from its parent in January 1974. By 1979 a Department of Prices and Consumer Affairs, and separate Departments of Trade and Industry had emerged. Similarly, a Department of Transport re-emerged from the DoE. None the less, when one takes into consideration the later re-absorption of some smaller departments, the general tendency over the period since 1970 was for a decline in the overall number of government departments and a relative increase in the significance of a few super-departments.

The idea that some aspects of civil service work could be carried out in agencies, as opposed to mainstream government departments, was not particularly new. Indeed, agencies had traditionally been set up in Britain on an *ad hoc* basis as a means of executing certain functions which required minimal ministerial involvement, or as channels for the delivery of expert advice to government. However, the Fulton Report broke new ground with its recommendation that a co-ordinated radical restructuring of government departments should take place, through 'hiving-off' some functions into new agencies. This theme was picked up in the Heath Government's 1970 White Paper, as a counter-balance to the concept of giantism.

In the event, only three major agencies were established: the Defence Procurement Executive was spawned by the Ministry of Defence; the Property Services Agency by the Department of the Environment; and the Manpower Services Commission (MSC) by the Department of Employment. Only in the latter did officials briefly lose their civil service status (between 1974 and 1976). These agencies were headed by Chairmen, appointed by the Secretaries of State in the parent departments, and were charged with delivering specific services to, respectively, the armed forces, government departments as a whole and the unemployed. They had substantial responsibility for their own budgets (in the case of the MSC, the budget doubled in the late 1970s and early 1980s as it assumed control over a series of special programmes such as the £1 billion Youth Training Scheme), and remained constitutionally accountable to ministers while operating at arm's length from their parent departments. In many respects, they were forerunners of the Next Steps agencies of the 1980s and 1990s.

Giantism and hiving-off provide us with evidence of a penchant on the part of these governments for macro change. The micro variety can be discerned in the managerial innovations which were being introduced during the 1970s.

An embryonic form of performance management began to emerge in Whitehall as accountable units were set up within departments. In these, attempts were made to measure 'outputs' against 'inputs' (including finance) and reach some conclusions about the performance of officials. In areas where difficulties precluded the measurement of civil servants' performances in terms of 'outputs', Management by Objectives (MbO) could be introduced. This facilitated judgement of performance against a set of previously agreed targets.

These techniques owed much to theories and practices developed in the world of American business in the 1960s and transferred into parts of the British private sector. This was also true of the rational policy planning process which, in the context of the British civil service, became Programme Analysis and Review (PAR).

PAR was the epitome of applied rationality. It was an attempt to take the academic theories of Herbert Simon, the American rationalist, learn from the practical experience of the business corporations which had experimented with rational decision-making procedures, and graft the whole lot onto Whitehall departments.

Thus, the fundamental principles underpinning departmental pro-grammes were to be examined and compared with other possible priorities, perhaps emanating from elsewhere in the government. PARs would produce detailed comparative information designed to allow senior civil servants and ministers to make rational choices about the specific composition of their departmental programmes.

The managerialist wave represented by accountable manage-ment units, output measurement, Management by Objectives and PAR probably reached its peak in the mid-1970s. A number of factors combined to bring about the demise of the various schemes and procedures (some were allowed to die on the vine, some lin-gered on in diluted form, some, such as PAR in 1979, were eventu-ally officially discarded).

The circumstances of the time did not help. It was perhaps a little difficult for some civil servants and their ministers to take seriously what many of them considered to be managerial tinker-ing, while economic and political crisis after crisis engulfed British government in the 1970s. Beyond this, the predicted rewards which were to accrue from the adoption of these techniques and pro-cedures did not seem to be forthcoming, at least in the short term. More fundamentally, an element of official and, from 1974, politi-cal, resistance set in. Suspicions on the part of some senior civil servants that managerialism was, at least in part, a stick with which the 'amateur' (Fulton's term) civil service was to be beaten into shape, led to a less than wholehearted embrace of the new order. One official was to write of 'The Great Management Hoax' (Sisson, 1976). Official suspicions were combined with an element of political hostility as some ministers in the post-1974 Labour Governments cast doubt upon the applicability of business-orientated schemes to the world of government.

In brief, the official and political culture was not yet right for the introduction of managerialism. Without a general acceptance of the new creed within the civil service, and a demonstrable and sustained commitment from ministers, managerialist experiments seemed likely to come and go like the leaves on the trees.

Post-1979: a 'new' managerialism and radical restructuring

During the 1960s the American politician, and later President, Richard Nixon was repeatedly recreating his image. A 'new' Nixon seemed to appear with increasing regularity. It might be argued that the 'new' managerialism is a bit like the 'new' Nixon: under the surface substantially the same as the old model! Is there anything truly new under the sun?

Ostensibly, at least, three differences did exist between the 1980s model of managerialism and its predecessor. The scale of activities was greater, there was a more overt attempt to change organisational culture as well as techniques and processes, and there was real and sustained political weight behind the exercise. The micro changes of the early 1980s were to dovetail into the macro changes which followed, and once again, political backing was not negligible.

If Edward Heath's Whitehall 'revolution' was 'quiet', Margaret Thatcher's was a high-decibel affair. She came to power with a clearly stated admiration for the values of private-sector management, and a distinctly unfavourable view of the civil service. The latter stemmed partly from her own ministerial experience as Secretary of State for Education and Science between 1970 and 1974, and partly from her reading of Leslie Chapman's *Your Disobedient Servant*, a highly critical account of Whitehall waste and inefficiency written by a retired civil servant (Chapman, 1978).

The clearest possible indication of the new Prime Minister's intentions came when she immediately established an Efficiency Unit within her Private Office. This was headed by her special adviser on efficiency, Derek Rayner, who had pioneered innovative managerial systems with Marks and Spencer as well as serving a sabbatical as Edward Heath's business adviser at the Ministry of Defence between 1970 and 1972. The fact that Rayner and his unit were based in 10 Downing Street demonstrated the Prime Minister's commitment to the cause of managerial reform.

The Efficiency Unit launched a programme of 'scrutinies' across Whitehall, designed to achieve cost savings and greater value for money. In addition, by 1982 new management information systems were springing up, geared to the needs of departmental ministers, and a broad Financial Management Initiative had been introduced. Rayner's return to the private sector in 1983 (he was succeeded by Sir Robin Ibbs, and then by Sir Angus Fraser) did not blunt the Efficiency Unit's cutting edge. It continued to enjoy the backing of the Prime Minister as it spearheaded the 'next step' towards managerial change: thorough-going structural reform through the creation of executive agencies. Micro themes were not totally submerged by the wave of macro, structural reform stemming from the launching of Next Steps in 1988, however. Under the Major premiership, the Efficiency Unit (now led by Sir Peter Levene and located within the Office of Public Service and Science) remained in the vanguard, as programmes of market testing and contracting out swept across Whitehall departments and the agencies.

Let us now look more closely at the micro and macro changes of the 1980s and 1990s.

'Micro' changes

Efficiency scrutinies

The Efficiency Unit spearheaded a concentrated attempt to introduce greater 'value for money' (VFM) in the civil service. VFM remains a rather vague and ambiguous concept, but it has been broadly defined in terms of three components: economy, efficiency and effectiveness (the 'three Es'). The precise meaning of these components, and the relative weight to be attached to each of them in any given case, remain rather elusive. Derek Rayner certainly wished to bring about cost savings (economies) in the civil service, on behalf of his political mistress. 'Raynerism' was to be inextricably linked with the cost-cutting instincts of Thatcherism, but it was also designed to enhance efficiency by increasing 'outputs', and improve effectiveness by ensuring that the 'outputs' from any given departmental activity were achieving the desired results.

Raynerism operated at two levels simultaneously. At the first level, it was concerned with bringing about improvements in the management of very specific spheres of government activity. These might be largely internal activities, such as arrangements for purchasing office equipment or organising the flow of vital information to ministers. Alternatively, the activities could be to do with service-delivery or policy-implementation, such as arrangements for paying social security benefits or maintaining roads in winter. Some spheres of activity would be common to a number of, if not all, departments.

Stage 1: Area of departmental activity selected for scrutiny

Stage 2: Scrutineer (Principal from Department) selected

Stage 3: Scrutineer conducts fieldwork in Department while liaising with Efficiency Unit

Stage 4: Opportunities for cost savings, increased efficiency and effectiveness identified

Stage 5: Report with recommendations produced within ninety days

Stage 6: Report sent to Secretary of State and Efficiency Unit

Stage 7: Liaison between Department and Efficiency Unit converts report into action document

Stage 8: Solutions implemented within one year of Stage 1

Stage 9: Final implementation report sent by minister to Efficiency Unit within two years of Stage 1

Figure 3.3   Key stages of an efficiency scrutiny

At the second level, Raynerism sought to inculcate the lessons of these specific studies, thus achieving lasting reforms across the whole civil service. A suitable analogy here might be the spreading of small brush-fires (the Rayner scrutinies), which would spread rapidly to engulf an expanse of land (the civil service as a whole). Whitehall was to be ablaze with managerial reform within a few years.

The key tools of Raynerism were the scrutinies, which survived the departure of their progenitor in 1983 (he returned to Marks and Spencer) and continue to be utilised. Figure 3.3 sets out the key stages of a scrutiny.

Rayner saw that his programme could only succeed if the civil service took 'ownership' of the reforms: if the scrutinies were viewed as alien devices imposed from without, resistance could be guaranteed. Thus, the choice of activities to be scrutinised is left to departments themselves (proposals might emanate from ministers or senior officials), the scrutineer is a Principal from the host department, the final decision on how to respond to the scrutiny is for the minister, and implementation of remedial action is for the department itself. The role of the Efficiency Unit is that of catalyst and co-ordinator. Given its deliberately small size (normally around ten individuals, some seconded from within the civil service, some specialist 'outsiders'), the Unit's involvement is necessarily limited, albeit extremely important. The Unit agrees the basic terms of reference for each scrutiny, liaises with the scrutineers, checks on progress, offers comments on draft reports and validates the final reports and action documents. Although disagreements between the Efficiency Unit and the scrutineer on the one side, and the department on the other, are rare, these do occur occasionally (Holland, 1988: 8).

Working within a very tight timetable, the scrutineer adopts a questioning approach, identifying areas of waste, duplication and inefficiency, while formulating recommendations designed to overcome the problems identified and achieve greater value for money. The scrutineer's report is a concise summary, designed for ease of consumption by busy ministers and senior civil servants, and intended to be the basis for an action document. This sets out the department's formal response to the scrutiny, the agreed reforms, a target date for implementation, anticipated savings, and a plan for implementation (Holland, 1988: 7).

The number of scrutinies conducted multiplied exponentially: 155 had been carried out by the time Rayner departed in 1983, and a further 150 had been completed by the end of the following year. Although the pace slowed somewhat thereafter, the scrutinies are now firmly established as a permanent feature of civil service self-assessment.

What have they achieved? Up to a point, there is unanimity about the value of the efficiency scrutinies. In so far as they uncovered clear examples of waste and inefficiency, the scrutinies could only be applauded. Examples of scrutiny findings included the following:

- Thirty-four per cent of cases handled by the Forensic Science Service contributed little or nothing to police investigations.
- Government research scientists were breeding rats at a cost of £30 each, while commercial laboratories were selling them for £2.
- Delays in the processing of passport applications could be attributed to the organisational location of the Passport

Office (within the Foreign Office rather than the Home Office) and the use of an outmoded computer system.

- Administration of capital grants to farmers cost £40 for every £100 of grant.
- Administration of woodland grants cost £90 for every £100 of grant.

Beyond the agreement that such inefficiencies were simply crying out to be exposed, there has been a certain amount of debate about the overall impact of the Efficiency Unit's work. Let us examine the main elements of the debate.

The main arguments in favour of the Unit's achievements point to substantial savings generated through the implementation of scrutiny action documents, and lasting changes in civil service management resulting from the brush-fire effect, alluded to above.

The true nature of the financial savings is rather difficult to assess, partly due to a confusion between potential savings which would be achieved if the recommendations of scrutinies were implemented in full, and real savings actually achieved. The Efficiency Unit itself claimed to be identifying potential savings of £600 million per year by 1985 (Efficiency Unit, 1985), and argued that real savings achieved by 1986 totalled £950 million (Committee of Public Accounts, 1986). By the early 1990s, total claimed savings were in the range £1.5–2 billion (Brereton, 1992: 73). Broadly favourable analyses of the efficiency scrutinies were published by the National Audit Office (National Audit Office, 1986) and the Public Accounts Committee of the House of Commons (Committee of Public Accounts, 1986), although the PAC noted that the early scrutinies in particular seemed to lack any clear focus on effectiveness (the primary concern being economy).

The two clearest illustrations of specific efficiency scrutinies precipitating wider managerial change, in line with Rayner's initial objective, were the Department of the Environment scrutinies which led to the Whitehall-wide Financial Management Initiative (more on this below), and the advent of management information systems for ministers.

The latter originated in the DoE in 1979. The new Secretary of State, Michael Heseltine, was personally interested in the application of management techniques to government departments. He was concerned about the lack of proper systems for providing ministers and senior civil servants in his department with the data needed for rational decision-making, and he initiated one of the first Rayner scrutinies on this theme.

As a result, a new Management Information System for Ministers (MINIS) was established in the DoE, geared towards providing ministers and senior civil servants with detailed information about the cost and effectiveness of departmental programmes. Heseltine was convinced that MINIS facilitated accurate checks upon the matching of departmental resources to policy priorities, and he took the system with him to the MoD in 1983. Under the auspices of the Financial Management Initiative, all government departments were obliged to introduce MINIS-type systems.

If it can be shown that the efficiency scrutinies generated substantial cash savings and sparked off wider managerial changes, what are the more negative points made about the work of the Efficiency Unit?

The civil service trade unions, and indeed some senior officials, were rather sceptical about Raynerism, particularly in its early phase. Economy cuts justified by Rayner scrutinies simply seemed to be part of a broader strategy determined by Margaret Thatcher's antipathy towards the civil service and her stated desire to cut its size. The line between Raynerism and Thatcherism seemed to be blurred, at best. In the search for VFM, the first 'E', economy, seemed to matter above all. Clive Ponting, a former civil servant who supported many of Rayner's aims, came to be highly critical of the search for staff cuts and short-term financial savings: 'the civil service could certainly be said to have emerged leaner, but not necessarily fitter; it has been not so much slimmed down as hacked at around the edges' (Ponting, 1989: 68). Ponting's own experience leads us to other criticisms of the efficiency scrutinies.

As a young, potential high-flyer in the Ministry of Defence, Ponting was charged with scrutinising the system for supplying food to the armed forces. There was no record of the total cost of this system, and Ponting discovered spectacular instances of waste and inefficiency (Ponting, 1986: 215). He was asked to present his findings directly to the Prime Minister, and was awarded the OBE for his work. However, rivalries between the three branches of the armed forces and a degree of ministerial inertia blocked the reforms Ponting had recommended.

This illustrates the point that, however professional and apparently rational an efficiency scrutiny might be, it can come into conflict with political reality or a flawed implementation system.

Indeed, good private-sector managerial practice and rational theory are not enough in the world of government: an acute understanding of the art of the possible is vital. This can be illustrated most vividly with reference to the 1981 scrutiny which reached the eminently rational conclusion that the DHSS budget could benefit to the tune of £66 million per year if only social security benefits could be paid into bank accounts rather than through post office order books. Rational, but politically naive! The proposal precipitated widespread protests by claimants groups, trade unions, sub-postmasters (whose livelihoods depended on the fees received for paying benefits) and MPs for rural constituencies fearing the demise of the vital sub-post offices. As a result, the proposal was drastically scaled down in the implementation.

On occasions, there would seem to have been less excuse for delayed or limited implementation of reforms:

> The 'Achilles Heel' of the scrutiny exercise appears to be the implementation process. There is still evidence of considerable opposition to the scrutinies within the civil service. . . . Implementation can become 'damage limitation' – reducing to a minimum the changes made. (Holland, 1988: 19)

The Financial Management Initiative

As we have already seen, the Financial Management Initiative (FMI) emerged from the core of an efficiency scrutiny conducted in the Department of the Environment. It represents the clearest example of an isolated Rayner brush-fire spreading to engulf the whole of Whitehall.

Having notified the Treasury and Civil Service Select Committee of its general intention, the government formally launched the FMI (based on an outline drafted by the Efficiency Unit) in May 1982. The initiative was to be co-ordinated by a joint Treasury/Cabinet Office body, the Financial Management Unit (which later became the Joint Management Unit). The initial objectives of the FMI were set out in a White Paper, published in September 1982 (White Paper, 1982), and periodically updated thereafter.

What was the FMI all about? A management consultant who worked in the Efficiency Unit when the initiative was being developed, viewed the FMI in broad terms:

> the objectives laid down for the FMI go far wider than purely financial issues. In essence, the FMI is about far more than improving the quality of financial information within government departments; it is concerned with a fundamentally new approach to the management of central government operations. (Oates, 1988: 1)

The need to be slightly sceptical about claims for the novelty of managerial schemes has already been noted. The FMI was not 'fundamentally new': it built upon past and existing trends, and gave a spur to some extant initiatives (Jackson, 1988: vi). However, Oates correctly stressed the extra-financial implications of the FMI. This point was recognised by a close observer of Whitehall managerialism:

> For civil servants, the financial management initiative has come to symbolise all that has happened in the field of management change in the public sector. . . . It is a catch-all label commonly applied to all the current attempts to improve efficiency and effectiveness, such as importing commercial principles of management, improving the financial skills of civil servants, buying in goods and services through contracting-out rather than producing them in-house, and so on. (Richards, 1987: 22)

There was no FMI blueprint, to be imposed on all departments of state. Instead, departments were encouraged to develop their own FMI, within a broad framework established by the Treasury and the Cabinet Office (the imprint of Rayner could be discerned in this approach, embodying as it does a concern for decentralisation and departmental 'ownership' of the initiative). Each department developed its own FMI vocabulary, working arrangements and culture. Viewed generally, the common characteristics of the departmental FMIs were as follows:

- MINIS-style management information systems for senior civil servants and ministers.
- Financial information systems designed to allow ministers, senior civil servants and line managers to differentiate between programme expenditure (i.e. spending on services, policies) and administrative expenditure.
- Devolved budgeting, achieved through the setting up of cost

centres and the identification of accountable line managers with considerable delegated authority over budgets.

- Rational budgeting techniques, which allow fundamental questions to be raised about the basic principles underpinning spending priorities.
- Value for money testing on a regular basis.
- Performance indicators and output measures, designed to evaluate relative success in achieving specific objectives.

It now seems clear that, although it rolled on into the restructured civil service of the 1990s (it had been designed as just that type of rolling programme which would probably develop in different ways and at different rates in the various departments), the early phase of the FMI was something of a disappointment to the government. The adoption of rational budgetary systems was problematic (Whitehall was not unique in encountering practical difficulties with such schemes!), devolved budgets were introduced patchily, theoretical and practical problems were encountered with performance measurement.

Observers had different views about the causes of these problems. For some, parts of the FMI, like other elements of the new managerialism, were simply irrelevant to the challenges of management in government but were being wielded by a government keen to cut 'bureaucracy' rather than modernise the civil service (Ponting, 1989: 69). Others, while not denying the negative impact of the Thatcher Government's confrontational style, attributed the lacklustre results to the mode of managing the initiative and to the 'impoverished concept of management' (as a discipline with limited application and relevance in the civil service) which permeates Whitehall (Metcalf and Richards, 1990).

Whatever the explanation, the outcome was clear: 'the initiative has . . . failed to create more than small incremental improvements. There has been no quantum leap' (Richards, 1987: 40). The government's concurrence with such a conclusion was to be a significant contributory factor in the emergence of the Next Steps programme, as we shall see.

Market testing

The final aspect of micro change to be considered, before we turn our attention to the macro variety, concerns the introduction of competition to increasing areas of civil service activity.

During the 1980s, compulsory competitive tendering (CCT) was introduced in the National Health Service and in local government. Specified activities, such as catering, cleaning and refuse collection, were compulsorily put out to tender, with the contract for providing the service being awarded to the most competitive bid. In some cases, this would involve contracting out: giving the contract to a private company.

By comparison, the civil service was only marginally affected by these developments. The element of widespread compulsion was missing, and a relatively small number of fairly low-grade manual and clerical tasks were exposed to competitive tendering (averaging £25 million worth of work a year by the early 1990s).

In November 1991, the government published a White Paper, *Competing for Quality*, which set out plans for an expansion of competitive tendering throughout the public sector (White Paper, 1991). Now, the civil service was being treated in a similar fashion to the National Health Service (NHS) and local government, and the new wave of competition was to involve professional, 'white-collar', functions such as accountancy, legal and administrative support services, as well as the more traditional targets for CCT.

The First Report on the Citizen's Charter, published in November 1992, contained the full programme of departmental and executive agency activities to be subject to market testing (exposed to competitive tendering) by the end of September 1993. In total, these activities were valued at almost £1.5 billion (this represented a fiftyfold increase over the previous annual level of market testing in the civil service) and covered over 44,000 staff (Citizen's Charter, 1992: 58–64). This was to be the first phase of a rolling programme.

While the selection of activities to be market tested was left up to departments and agencies, the Efficiency Unit had a role in ensuring that suitable numbers of activities were being identified. Specifications for the contracts were drawn up, in-house bids encouraged, tenders sought through advertising, the tenders thoroughly evaluated and contracts awarded. In order to place themselves in a reasonable position to win a contract, an in-house team would probably have to undergo a rigorous process of self-appraisal, perhaps involving adjustments to conditions of service.

The market-testing procedures have to be seen to be entirely fair. Departmental and agency evaluation teams manage the tendering process and award the contracts (not necessarily to the

Table 3.1   Market testing in two departments

Department: Social Security
Targets (1992):
Value of activities to be tested: £127 million
Posts covered: 6,900
Activities to be tested:
    accommodation and office services
    accountancy services
    archival storage
    audit
    catering
    data entry
    legal services
    medical services and administrative support
    resettlement centres
    training
Results (1993):
Value of activities tested: £15 million
Posts covered: 490
Activities tested:
    accommodation and office services
    audit
    data entry
    training

Department: Employment
Targets (1992):
Value of activities to be tested: £72 million
Posts covered: 1,900
Activities to be tested:
    central despatch
    employment rehabilitation courses
    estates services
    IT support of non-mainframe applications
    Jobclubs/Jobsearch seminars
    payroll services
    pensions administration
    publications distribution
    reprographics
    security
    typing services
Results (1993):
Value of activities tested: £46.9 miilion
Posts covered: 1,021
Activities tested:
    central despatch
    employment rehabilitation courses

continued

estates services
Jobclubs
publications distribution
reprographics
security
typing services

Sources: Citizen's Charter, *First Report, 1992; Second Report, 1994.*

lowest bidders, although there have to be strong arguments for failing to do this). 'Chinese walls', or organisational divisions, must be established to ensure a strict separation of in-house bidders and the evaluation teams.

Once the contract is awarded, a system for monitoring the quality, cost-effectiveness and contract compliance of the contractor (even if this is the in-house team) is required. Penalties may be applied in cases of non-compliance, and, in extreme cases, contracts may be ended, but this can only be done if the department or agency has set out the consequences of non-compliance in a clear and detailed fashion, in advance.

The results of the first wave of market testing were a disappointment for the government, although the problems were rather glossed over in the official review of the exercise, which claimed savings of 'at least £135 million' (Citizen's Charter, 1994: 93–109). Table 3.1 sets out the impact of market testing on two departments during the period until the end of December 1993. Overall, the government fell far short of realising its target of testing £1.5 billion worth of activities by 30 September 1993. Less than half of this amount had been examined by the deadline, although the figure had risen to £1.1 billion by the end of December that year. Table 3.2 summarises some of the main general results of the first wave of tests. However disappointed it might have been, the government remained committed to market testing, and announced partially revised targets for future rounds of the process (Citizen's Charter, 1994; Stott, 1994).

While it will take some time for the long-term impact of market testing to be fully evaluated, it is possible to summarise the key elements of the debate which has surrounded the entire exercise.

The government argued that market testing was the next logical stage in the search for greater value for money. William

Table 3.2   The 1992–3 market-testing programme

	Number	Percentage
Tests	389	100.00
Activities abolished	25	6.43
Activities privatised	3	0.77
Activities restructured	6	1.54
Tests halted and efficiency gains made instead	13	3.34
Contracted out (without in-house bid)	113	29.05
Contracted out (with in-house bid)	82	21.08
Contract won by in-house team	147	37.79

Source: Citizen's Charter, *Second Report, 1994.*

Waldegrave, the Chancellor of the Duchy of Lancaster until July 1994, who, as political head of the Office of Public Service and Science, had initial responsibility for the entire programme, stated the government's case:

> Our aim is not a dogmatic adherence to a particular philosophy, but a better deal for the taxpayer, the user of the services, and, we hope, for the employees. If the private sector is to win, they will need to offer better value for money than the existing in-house oper-ation. . . . Although the White Paper sets clear targets for the amount of government activity which is to be market tested, there are no targets for the amount which is to be contracted out. So there is not some sort of hidden agenda – privatisation by the back door. (Waldegrave, 1993: 5)

However, such arguments were not accepted uncritically. Severe reservations were expressed by the civil service trade unions (who organised strikes against contracting out in November 1993), the opposition parties, and, to some extent, even by senior officials.

Certain ministers, including the President of the Board of Trade, Michael Heseltine, and the Social Security Secretary, Peter Lilley, were apparently dragging their feet over this issue. They spec-tacularly failed to meet their targets for market testing, although, perversely, they managed to spend more than any of their col-leagues (a total of £8 million) on management consultants offering advice on how to implement market testing (Hencke, 1994).

Close observers of Whitehall could detect the emergence of strains between the Efficiency Unit and the Next Steps Team on the subject of market testing. After all, surely the whole point of

Next Steps was the delegation of managerial freedoms to Chief Executives? What did this amount to if they were obliged to subject their agencies to precisely the same market-testing regime as conventional departments? Before long, press reports began to appear about the disenchantment of some Chief Executives with the handling of market testing (Hencke, 1993).

The unions feared that the government did have a hidden agenda, a built-in bias in favour of contracting work out to the private sector, and no 'level playing field' which would allow in-house teams a fair chance of winning contracts. They argued that the market-testing process would be costly and administratively cumbersome. Contracting out would bring job losses, poorer conditions of service (although there were some hopes that test cases using the EU 'Acquired Rights' Directive would guarantee continuance of existing terms and conditions), lower standards of service, problems of security and confidentiality (particularly in relation to the contracting out of information technology and computing services), and risks of corruption (First Division Association, 1992; 1993a; 1993b; Labour Research, 1993).

The results of the first wave of market testing provided some support for at least certain elements of the unions' case. The private sector was awarded £855 million worth of contracts, and £768 million of this was won without competition from in-house teams, because the latter were not permitted to bid. Where they were allowed to compete, the in-house teams won 68 per cent of the work, amounting to £189 million (Citizen's Charter, 1994: 93). Out of over 25,000 posts subjected to testing, 14,500 were lost (Citizen's Charter, 1994: 101).

Hovering over the entire exercise was a concern about the possible loss of the public service ethos, and the ultimate disintegration of the civil service. Clearly, the market-testing initiative is at a relatively early stage, and the results of successive waves of the process have to be closely analysed before such a conclusion could be reached. The government's basic contention is that a general programme of market testing, which will result in an element of contracting out, poses no threat to the cohesion of the civil service. If major private-sector companies can contract out their peripheral services such as reprographics and computing without losing their corporate identities, why cannot the civil service? Opponents argue that the type of work being market tested goes beyond peripheral activities, and a sensible search for greater value for money has been undermined by the injection of political dogma.

'Macro' changes

The structural reforms introduced in the civil service from the late 1980s were on a scale which dwarfed the tinkerings of the 1960s and 1970s. Indeed, they quickly came to be seen as the most significant changes attempted since the days of Northcote and Trevelyan. In a very real sense, these macro changes emerged out of the micro changes analysed above, while giving a fresh impetus to elements of the new managerialism.

As the broad structural and managerial implications of Next Steps are set out, it should be borne in mind that the advent of executive agencies had wider repercussions for accountability, policy formation and implementation, as well as the minister–civil servant relationship. These themes are covered in other chapters.

The Ibbs Report

Derek Rayner's successor as special adviser to the Prime Minister on efficiency, Robin Ibbs, became concerned about the apparent failure of the Financial Management Initiative to bring about fundamental change in the civil service. In an attempt to review the managerial changes which had taken place, identify the obstacles to further change and clear the way for greater improvements in efficiency, Ibbs gave a small team from the Efficiency Unit a special commission. They were to produce a report for the Prime Minister.

In November 1986, Kate Jenkins, Karen Caines and Andrew Jackson embarked on a project which was to include fieldwork in departments of state, government agencies and leading private-sector organisations (including ICI and the Halifax Building Society), as well as interviews with over 150 ministers and senior civil servants and formal meetings with the Council of Civil Service Unions. In true Efficiency Unit style, the resulting report, *Improving Management in Government: The next steps* was delivered within a strict timetable: it was with the Prime Minister in the spring of 1987.

Although amendments were made to the report before it was finally published the following year, the Ibbs Report (Efficiency Unit, 1988) remained a bold document. Its implicit conclusion was that the Thatcher managerial reforms had failed to transform the civil service, and fundamental structural reform would be necessary in order to achieve lasting managerial change. The basic problem was seen to be the sheer scale of the civil service, which was

> too big and too diverse to manage as a single entity. . . . A single organisation of this size which attempts to provide a detailed structure within which to carry out functions as diverse as driver licensing, fisheries protection, the catching of drug smugglers and the processing of Parliamentary Questions is bound to develop in a way which fits no single operation effectively. (Efficiency Unit, 1988: para. 10)

The existing obstacles to lasting managerial change could only be overcome if the executive functions of government departments were carried out through new agencies, operating at arm's length from their parent departments. In some cases, whole blocks of departmental work might be assigned to an agency, in others, multiple agencies would emerge from the old monolith.

Some critics viewed Next Steps as a stalking horse for large-scale privatisation. The government argued that this was not the initiative's primary goal, although it might emerge as an option when departments initially reviewed their activities and programmes, or later, when an agency had been operating for a number of years and its role could be reconsidered. Two agencies were specifically earmarked for privatisation from the outset (the National Engineering Laboratory and ADAS, the agricultural consultancy agency), while for two others (DVOIT, an information technology agency, and Companies House) the decision to privatise was taken after a period of operating as agencies.

The overall implications of Next Steps were clear. The report's authors estimated that 95 per cent of the civil service deals with service delivery and implementation (executive functions), so the creation of agencies could transform the shape of the entire service. Policy formation would take place in small, core or parent departments, but these would be very different from the conventional departments of state, which would effectively be broken up into executive agencies and cores. Although most of the subsequent attention focused on the concept of executive agencies, it was clear that Ibbs' proposals had potentially important implications for the environment within which the higher civil service functioned. It seemed likely that fewer mandarins would be required in Whitehall, and their traditional working practices would be exposed to the winds of the new managerialism.

The report recommended that the agencies should be headed by Chief Executives, who would be given significant managerial freedoms (over recruitment, salaries and gradings) and made accountable to Parliament as well as to their departmental ministers back in the parent departments.

In the period leading up to publication of a revised version of the report, there were rumours of fairly serious Whitehall in-fighting, with the Treasury in particular apparently fearful that its traditional dominance over civil service affairs was at risk (Drewry, 1988c). The circumstances surrounding the programme's formal launching suggested that at least some of the potential radicalism of Ibbs had been toned down.

The Next Steps programme

Margaret Thatcher announced her government's intention to implement the Ibbs Report in a Commons statement on 18 February 1988 (Thatcher, 1988), while stressing the Treasury's continuing authority over strategic pay, personnel and budgetary matters, and denying the need for alterations to the existing constitutional arrangements for accountability.

The Prime Minister threw her weight behind the initiative and appointed Peter Kemp, formerly a senior Treasury official, as Project Manager, charged with co-ordinating the entire exercise. Kemp operated from within the Cabinet Office, and headed a unit of around a dozen civil servants. He was abruptly dismissed in 1992 when the unit was refashioned as the Next Steps and Management Development Group, located in the new Office of Public Service and Science (under a new Permanent Secretary, Richard Mottram). Although Kemp had managed Next Steps with flair and energy, he was known to have some reservations about the market-testing programme, and he came into conflict with William Waldegrave. In an extremely unusual development, Sir Robin

Butler, the Head of the Civil Service, was unable to offer Kemp an alternative post, and he was obliged to leave.

The Next Steps programme was launched with an announcement that twelve candidates for agency status had been identified, employing a total of 70,000 people. Only the prospective Employment Service Agency seemed to be of much political significance (it contained 35,000 officials, including those working in Jobcentres), and the scale of this programme was compared unfavourably with the radical tone of the Ibbs Report. The programme got off to a rather slow start. The first agency, the Vehicle Inspectorate, was launched in August 1988, but only twelve agencies had been established by March 1990. Was this yet another reform which had been neutralised by the Treasury and other vested interests? Peter Kemp sought to rebut this suggestion by claiming that at least 75 per cent of the civil service would be operating on Next Steps lines by the year 2000 (Treasury and Civil Service Committee, 1988a).

As the programme developed, it quickly became clear that a fundamental macro reform, restructuring the entire civil service, was indeed in progress.

By the summer of 1994, over 264,000 civil servants were working in 97 Next Steps agencies. Once the numerous executive units and offices of the Inland Revenue and Customs and Excise were taken into consideration, nearly 350,000 civil servants, 60 per cent of the total, were working in executive agencies. A further 56 agency candidates, employing nearly 93,879 officials, had been identified by ministers and the aim was to have established virtually all agencies by the middle of 1995 (Next Steps Team, 1994).

Although some agencies are extremely small and of only marginal significance (the Wilton Park Conference Centre employs only 30 people), many operate in vital areas of government activity. Defence operational analysis and research, employment services, social security benefits, agricultural intervention, the prison service, and RAF logistics and signals support are among the functions handled by agencies. The Fraser Report, an Efficiency Unit review of Next Steps' first three years, identified four categories of agency (Efficiency Unit, 1991: Annex A):

- *Mainstream:* central to the policy and operation of their departments, such as the Employment Service and the Social Security Benefits Agencies.

- *Regulatory and other statutory agencies:* execute statutory functions derived from the main aims of their department, such as the Vehicle Inspectorate.
- *Specialist service agencies:* provide internal services to their departments or to other agencies, like the DSS Information Technology Services Agency.
- *Peripheral:* not linked to any of the main aims of their departments, such as Historic Royal Palaces.

Organisational and managerial impact

Figure 3.4 shows the basic procedure for the establishment of a Next Steps agency. The process of examining departmental activities and programmes with a view to deciding where there is scope for improved management could precipitate fundamental restructuring. Take the example of the Department of Social Security.

By 1994, the parent DSS had spawned six executive agencies (Benefits, Child Support, Contributions, Information Technology Services, Resettlement and War Pensions) which collectively employ over 98 per cent of Social Security officials (Greer, 1994: 32). The Benefits Agency, as the largest Next Steps agency of all, employs nearly 65,000 staff, dispenses £62 billion of public money in benefits and has running costs of £1.9 billion (Chancellor of the Duchy of Lancaster, 1993; Next Steps Team, 1994).

In this simple sense, the organisational impact of Next Steps can be highly significant. However, the purpose of the initiative went beyond redrawing the bureaucratic map. New types of civil service managers, armed with managerial freedom, were to take the agencies into a new world of efficiency. In the meantime, the parent departments would be able to redesign themselves and focus on their specialist strengths.

In the period since Next Steps was launched, a range of official reports, surveys by management consultants and academic commentaries have examined the accumulating evidence. The picture remains rather confused, and it is impossible to reach a definitive verdict on the managerial impact of the initiative, but some themes are emerging.

Ministers were to decide on the most appropriate method of selecting Chief Executives for the agencies associated with their

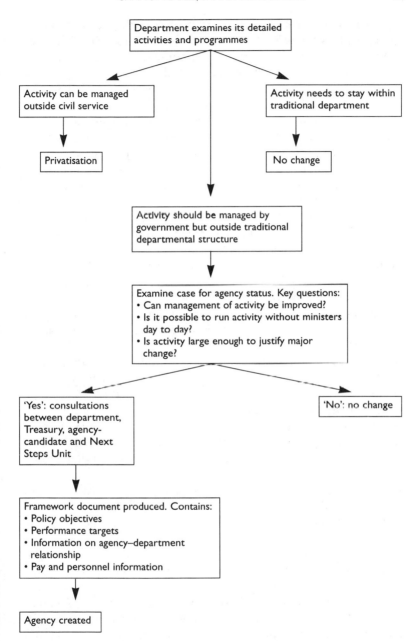

Figure 3.4 Setting up a Next Steps agency

departments: internal selection (from within the department, or service-wide) or external selection via open competition. The government did not wish to make open competitions mandatory for these appointments, but took the view that they should 'become the conventional route to these posts' (Treasury and Civil Service Committee, 1990b: 8). In the event, as we saw in Chapter 2, the selection procedures for agency Chief Executives came to be seen as the shape of things to come elsewhere in the civil service. Of 100 Chief Executive and Chief Executive designate appointments made by the summer of 1994, 69 were recruited via open competition, and 37 of these came from outside the civil service (Next Steps Team, 1994).

Once in post, the Chief Executives were charged with the task of managing their agencies, and were given a considerable amount of, but not unlimited, freedom. The Framework Documents set out the nature of the managerial autonomy given to the Chief Executives, who were required to produce annual reports specifying the extent to which agreed targets had been met.

Basically, they would enjoy the maximum power possible over the appointment, payment and disciplining of their staffs, within existing civil service guidelines and standards. Of course, the latter were themselves becoming more loose and flexible than heretofore. Thus, performance-related pay schemes, special responsibility allowances and special rates of pay for certain appointees, were all feasible. The largest agencies assumed responsibility for their own pay bargaining in the spring of 1994. Even greater financial autonomy was enjoyed by those agencies designated as Trading Funds, which were not financed through the parliamentary 'vote' of their parent department.

The culture of the agencies was avowedly that of private-sector business. In addition to the influx of outsiders as Chief Executives (although it should be noted that some of these, including the Chief Executive of the Benefits Agency, came from elsewhere in the public sector), the agencies had management boards containing representatives from the world of business and operated in an environment of corporate plans, business plans and annual reports.

Three years into the initiative, the Fraser Report (Efficiency Unit, 1991) argued for greater 'empowering' of Chief Executives, since, at that stage, many parent departments appeared to be unwilling to delegate to the fullest possible extent, and the volume of contact between departments and agencies was extremely high. As a result, Framework Documents were to be revised periodically, and the exclusion of any area from the jurisdiction of Chief Executives fully justified. Regular surveys by the management consultants Price Waterhouse confirmed a concern on the part of Chief Executives about the demands of parent departments specifically, and the central management of the civil service generally (Price Waterhouse, 1991: 9; 1992: 6–8).

Fraser also took aim at the apparent lack of change in operations and staffing levels in the parent departments (after all, the initiative was meant to bring about change in the policy-making core departments as well as the executive agencies).

The drive for increased agency autonomy had another aspect, however. The civil service unions, the Treasury and Civil Service Select Committee, and some senior mandarins, expressed concerns during the advent of Next Steps, and from time to time thereafter, about the impact of structural Balkanisation and wide-ranging managerial freedoms on career opportunities and mobility. Would officials be consigned for the duration of their working lives to the 'ghetto' of an agency, cut adrift from its parent department and the rest of the civil service by its organisational location and its very particular pay schemes and conditions of service?

While emphasising its continuing commitment to staff transfers within the civil service, the government maintained that precedence must be given to the jobs to be done and finding the right people for those jobs (Treasury and Civil Service Committee, 1991b: 7). In other words, career opportunities and mobility, while desirable, were not of primary importance.

From a unitary to a federal model

Among the numerous themes which have run through this chapter, one emerges with reasonable clarity. The micro and macro changes set out here represent a substantial move away from the concept of a centralised, unitary civil service, towards an organisation containing a multiplicity of fairly discrete component parts, within which managers have significant freedom for manoeuvre. A gradual but developing delegation of managerial authority, together with the major structural reform represented by Next Steps moulded the civil service into a new shape, with its own distinctive characteristics.

What seemed to be emerging out of the old unitary body was a federation, still bound together through the links between parent departments and agencies and by the remaining adherence to civil service standards and norms, but with the potential for distinctive modes of behaviour and organisation to develop within the individual entities of the federal model.

The Civil Service (Management Functions) Act of 1993 provided clear evidence of this move away from the unitary and towards the federal model. This Act empowered the Treasury and the Office of Public Service and Science to delegate the management functions which they exercise to other servants of the Crown. Thus, the path was opened to the specific delegation of functions to particular departments or agencies, or the general delegation of functions to all departments and agencies. It had become possible for the component parts of this federal civil service to be given a free hand to determine an extremely wide range of terms and conditions of service without reference to the centre.

The nature of the federal bond, and the fundamental question about whether Britain was effectively going to have, not a civil service, but many civil services, sparked off a debate, to which we will return in the concluding chapter.

In this wide-ranging chapter we have charted the changing size and shape of the civil service and noted the impact of waves of managerial and structural change. Many of the themes and topics will arise again as we examine the implementation of policy and the 'quality' issue in Chapter 5 and turn our attention to matters of accountability in Chapter 6. For the time being, however, it would be appropriate at this stage to focus on the policy dimension of civil service work.

4

SERVING THE CENTRAL EXECUTIVE

The purpose of this chapter is to give some consideration to the role of the civil service in the sphere of policy formation and decision-making, and to examine issues associated with this aspect of serving the central executive.

Ministers, civil servants and policy

The doctrine of individual ministerial responsibility ascribes a range of key roles to government ministers (Pyper, 1987a). They can be said to be responsible for the following:

- Policy leadership in their departments.
- Managing departments.
- Piloting legislation through its various parliamentary stages.
- Acting as ambassadors, or advocates, when representing departmental interests in Cabinet, with pressure/interest groups and departmental clients.

As we have already seen, the roles of civil servants can be similarly categorised as involving the administration or implementation of policy, departmental or agency management, and the provision of policy advice to ministers. It is the latter role which is our main concern here.

Put simply, the doctrine of individual ministerial responsibility envisages the creation of policy by ministers, on the advice of their officials. As we shall see, this is a rather limited interpretation of the policy and decision-making processes. These are considerably more subtle and complex than the mechanistic 'civil servants advise, ministers decide' formula would lead us to believe. However, we have established a useful starting point by recognising one of the civil servant's roles as that of policy adviser. It is a role primarily, although not exclusively, undertaken by the most senior officials, operating in the ranks of the Open Structure.

The policy relationship between ministers and officials

The working relationship between ministers and civil servants in the sphere of policy formation can be affected by a wide range of formal and informal factors. This can be illustrated with reference to eight variables.

The first of these is the nature of ministerial life. As we have seen, government ministers perform four reasonably clear roles in their ministerial capacity. Additionally, most ministers have seats in the House of Commons, and must attend to the constituency responsibilities associated with this status. All ministers are party politicians, and operate in this capacity, to a greater or lesser degree, at parliamentary, national and local levels. The net effect of all this is that ministers, in contrast with their civil servants, perform tasks which may take them outside their departments for up to two-thirds of the normal working week (Headey, 1974: 187).

A second variable is ministerial tenure. While some ministers spend extended periods of time in particular posts (the Chancellorships of Denis Healey in the 1970s and Geoffrey Howe in the 1980s spring to mind), and develop mature policy relationships with their senior officials, it is more normal for departments to witness a fairly steady turnover of ministerial personnel, resulting in a degree of discontinuity.

The third variable concerns the manner in which the formal constitutional proprieties are observed by ministers and civil servants alike. The policy relationship between a team of ministers and the senior civil servants in a department is hedged around with procedural and behavioural niceties. The rule book of ministerial conduct, *Questions of Procedure for Ministers* (Cabinet Office,

1992), makes it clear that the Permanent Secretary's formal relationship is to the Secretary of State, to whom there is a clear duty to advise on matters of policy. The relationship between a Permanent Secretary and other members of a ministerial team is more problematic, however, as Madgwick and Woodhouse (1993) have shown, with reference to *Questions of Procedure*:

> The Permanent Secretary . . . is not subject to the directions of junior ministers. . . . The lines are delicately drawn. The Permanent Secretary's 'keep off my patch!' is nicely phrased as 'that does not relieve me of my responsibilities.' But if junior ministers (the 'junior' puts them in their place) sometimes get uppity, Permanent Secretaries are warned: 'junior ministers are not subject to the direction of the Permanent Secretary.' (Madgwick and Woodhouse, 1993: 39)

While ministers are expected to give reasonable consideration to the policy advice given by civil servants, they are not obliged to accept this advice. It is comparatively rare for policy disagreements between ministers and officials to become public, but there was an instance of this in the autumn of 1993 when the 'vigorous' debates on law and order policy between the Home Secretary, Michael Howard, and his civil servants, were widely reported, and commented upon by Howard (Travis, 1993). As we shall argue below, in a slightly different context, vigorous exchanges of views between ministers and their officials can be more healthy for all concerned than meek civil service compliance.

Our fourth variable has to do with the personalities and working habits of particular ministers and civil servants. It is easy to ignore the impact of such matters on the policy relationship, but the interaction between dominant (not to say domineering!) figures such as Dame Evelyn Sharp on the civil service side and Richard Crossman on the ministerial side (they were respectively, Permanent Secretary and Secretary of State at the Ministry of Housing and Local Government, 1964–6, and their stormy relationship was vividly described in Crossman's *Diaries*) can be highly significant. The highly conflictual working relationship typified by Crossman and Sharp can be contrasted with others, characterised by detachment or collegiality (Pyper, 1991: 37).

A fifth variable is the relative knowledge and expertise a minister brings to his or her departmental tasks. While new ministers may possess clear and practicable policy ideas as a result of their professional or political backgrounds, this is by no means certain. Ministers are not invariably posted to particular departments because of their grasp of, or even interest in, a specific policy sphere, and this can have an effect on the policy relationship with civil servants. Alan Clark's reaction to his initial workload as Parliamentary Under Secretary of State for Employment was disarmingly honest:

> Faster than I can digest them great wadges of documentation are whumped into my 'In' tray. The subject matter is turgid: a mass of 'schemes' . . . the Enterprise Allowance Scheme, the Job Release Scheme, the Community Scheme. Convoluted and obscure even at their inception, they have since been so picked over and 'modified' by civil servants as to be incomprehensible. I ought to welcome these devices, and must try and master their intricacies. But my head is bursting. (Clark, 1993: 9–10)

The sixth variable relates to the political 'weight' of the Secretary of State. The policy relationship between a minister possessing significant clout in the Cabinet and the party, and his or her senior civil servants, can have quite a different character from that between a relatively insignificant minister and his or her officials. Of course, it should be remembered that ministerial careers can be fairly volatile; peaks of high status and prestige may be followed by troughs of low influence, and vice versa.

Just as the importance of ministers can vary over time, so too the significance of particular departments of state in relation to the overall strategy of a government is subject to a certain amount of change, and this presents us with a seventh variable. The Treasury, the Foreign Office and, to some extent, the Home Office, remain central to the strategy of most governments, but the pecking order of the other departments can alter, even within the lifetime of a government, and this is likely to have an effect both on the ministers appointed to specific posts, and on the policy relationships between ministers and officials.

Finally, if the importance of ministers and of departments is subject to change over time, the significance attached to departmental policy can also vary markedly. During any given period, a department may represent something of a policy backwater, with relatively minor initiatives occupying the time of ministers and senior civil servants. However, a department, its ministers and officials can be charged (sometimes unexpectedly) with responsibility for developing a 'flagship' policy, carrying with it the hopes of the government itself.

Manipulating, serving, or being manipulated?

It can be seen from the above that civil servants enjoy several advantages over ministers when proffering policy advice. The cumulative effect of these, in the eyes of some observers and politicians, is to facilitate a 'dictatorship of the official', or allow civil service 'conspiracies' to undermine the wishes of their ministers.

From their very different political perspectives, some people from both the right and the left of British politics have subscribed to this interpretation of civil service power and manipulation, arguing that senior officials have a natural aversion to radical initiatives, and an inherent proclivity in favour of centrist, consensus policies.

The leftist viewpoint is that the higher civil service is effectively part of the establishment, in terms of its social composition and collective outlook. It acts as an arm of the ruling class in maintaining the *status quo* while diluting the radical initiatives of Labour Governments in general, and ideologically committed ministers such as Tony Benn in particular (Kellner and Crowther-Hunt, 1980: *passim*; Sedgemore, 1980: *passim*; Benn, 1982: Chapter 3; 1990: *passim*).

The rightist viewpoint is that the period since 1945 saw the civil service become inextricably linked into the culture of 'big' government. It became comfortable with, and a part of, the so-called post-war consensus, and was wedded to the orthodoxies of economic and social intervention. In this interpretation, Whitehall had effectively become part of a 'socialist' or 'social democratic' establishment (Hoskyns, 1983; Hennessy, 1989a: Chapter 15; Young, 1990: Chapter 9).

These interpretations can serve as healthy antidotes to a bland, uncritical view of the civil service as an unswervingly neutral institution, and they can offer fresh insights into the policy relationship between ministers and civil servants. However, it is not necessary to accept either of them in its entirety in order to obtain these benefits.

One significant difference between these two points of view was that the Labour Prime Ministers Harold Wilson and James Callaghan never shared the suspicions of the civil service expressed by some of their own ministers (Tony Benn in particular), while Margaret Thatcher clearly aligned herself with the rightist critique of Whitehall. This led some commentators and politicians to conclude that she used her influence to bring about sweeping changes in personnel at the top of the civil service. The facts of this matter deserve some scrutiny.

In a sense, Margaret Thatcher was extremely fortunate. She was Prime Minister just at the time when a large number of senior civil servants were reaching retirement. Hennessy (1988) points out that 43 Permanent Secretaries and 138 Deputy Secretaries retired between 1979 and 1985. The net effect of this was that a very large number of vacancies had to be filled in the top grades of the Open Structure. Where previous premiers had usually adopted a fairly relaxed approach to civil service appointments, giving final approval to nominations forwarded by the Senior Appointments Selection Committee, Margaret Thatcher took pains to make her preferences clear to the Committee, through its chairman, the Cabinet Secretary. Sir Robert Armstrong was left in no doubt about the individuals the PM wished to see promoted, and a certain degree of controversy surrounded some of the appointments (including the promotions of Clive Whitmore and Peter Middleton to the Permanent Secretaryships at the Ministry of Defence and the Treasury, respectively).

There were fears that the top ranks of the civil service were being 'politicised' by stealth, in the search for a certain type of committed service. For a time, it seemed that the Labour Party might be prepared to launch a purge, should it be returned to power. In 1989 Dr John Cunningham, a senior member of the Shadow Cabinet, spoke about the need to

> look closely at what's been happening in Whitehall. . . . We've seen Mrs. Thatcher pursue the 'one of us' syndrome right across the whole administration in this country including the civil service. And I think there must be a number of people in Whitehall now in senior positions who are, frankly, compromised by that – and they'd have to go. (Quoted in Hennessy, 1989b)

This line was subsequently softened somewhat. Partly, this was because the Opposition came to recognise the validity of what the most astute Whitehall observers, such as Peter Hennessy, had been saying all along: the 'Thatcher appointments' were characterised by a bias in favour of a certain type of individual, rather than an examination of appointees' party political preferences. While making due allowance for his natural partiality, it is worth recounting the view of William Waldegrave on this matter:

> I think people systematically misrepresented what Mrs. Thatcher was interested in in the appointments she made. She did have a sort of preferred model of people she liked to appoint – it was nothing to do with party. What she liked was activist, extrovert people. So there was a bias in that direction, if you like, about a certain kind of personality on an Eysenck scale or something. But it was nothing to do with politicisation. (Quoted in Hennessy and Coates, 1992: 8)

The Labour Party's approach was possibly also influenced by the sensitivity shown to its views in the period leading up to the 1992 General Election. Even before the conventional, highly discreet pre-election meetings between Whitehall Permanent Secretaries and Shadow Ministers, the Labour leadership was actually sounded out by the Cabinet Secretary (with the knowledge of the Prime Minister) on the appointment of a new Permanent Secretary to the Treasury (Hennessy and Coates, 1992: 5). In April 1991, Neil Kinnock and John Smith (at that time, respectively, Leader of the Opposition and Shadow Chancellor) were content to see Sir Terence Burns, the government's Chief Economic Adviser, appointed to the post. Given that Burns had been plucked from an academic post at the London Business School in 1979 to serve the Thatcher Government as a monetarist guru, he might have been seen as inherently unacceptable to Labour, but this was not the case. Burns would have been given his chance to serve a new Labour Government, had one been elected the following year. To summarise, talk of a Whitehall purge, or the removal of 'damaged goods' sharply receded in the 1990s.

None the less, it would be complacent to conclude from this that no harm was done by the interventionist Thatcherite approach to appointments, or indeed, to assert that four successive Conservative election victories has had a neutral impact on the quality of service provided by the most senior civil servants in the realm of policy advice.

William Waldegrave's remarks, partly cited above, went on to laud the actions of officials in helping ministers firstly to construct, then to dismantle, the policy on the Community Charge. This, and similar cases, could equally be seen as evidence of the inability of civil servants, imbued with the ethos of entrenched Conservative government, to play their full and proper role as policy advisers. As Peter Hennessy shrewdly commented, 'No wonder Mr. Waldegrave, like Mrs. Thatcher, thought having energetic civil servants mattered. And does such professional compliance illustrate the possibility of limited mind sets . . . ?' (Hennessy and Coates, 1992: 8). This point has been developed by William Plowden, who cites instances of policy failure which can be attributed to the inability or unwillingness of senior civil servants to proffer frank advice, for fear of damaging their career prospects. Plowden points out that 'artificial' agreement with ministers, and 'suppression of intellectual dissent' can be profoundly damaging for the process of government (Plowden, 1994: 102–9).

When their service is over: the ethics of post-retirement jobs

The detailed policy work carried out by senior civil servants makes them extremely attractive to many private-sector employers. It has become increasingly common for retired officials to take up lucrative jobs in business and commerce on retirement from the civil service. The most prominent examples (see Pallister and Norton-Taylor, 1992a) include the following:

- Lord Bancroft, Head of the Home Civil Service until 1981, who became a director of the Rugby Group, Bass, Grindlays Bank, ANZ Merchant Bank and deputy chairman of the Sun Life Corporation.
- Lord Hunt of Tanworth, Secretary to the Cabinet until 1979, who went on to become chairman of the Prudential Corporation, IBM (UK), Unilever, the Banque Nationale de Paris and a director of Tablet Publishing and BNP UK Holdings.
- Sir Douglas Wass, Permanent Secretary to the Treasury and joint Head of the Home Civil Service until 1983, who became chairman of the Japanese bank Nomura International, and of Equity and Law, as well as being a director of Barclays Bank, and De Le Rue Company and a consultant for Coopers and Lybrand.
- Lord Armstrong of Ilminster, Secretary to the Cabinet and Head of the Home Civil Service until 1987, who took up the

chairmanship of BAT Industries, and directorships with the Bristol and West Building Society, Biotechnology Investments, Lucas Industries, NM Rothschild and Sons, RTZ Corporation and Shell Transport and Trading.

- Sir Peter Middleton, Permanent Secretary to the Treasury until 1991, became deputy chairman of Barclays Bank, chairman of Barclays de Zoete Wedd.

The journalists David Pallister and Richard Norton-Taylor discovered that 60 per cent of all retiring senior civil servants and armed forces officers can expect to hold up to six directorships within six months of leaving their old posts (Pallister and Norton-Taylor, 1992b).

The government's rules about the 'revolving door' of post-retirement appointments have been updated periodically, in order to strike a balance between preserving the freedom of former civil servants to pursue new careers, facilitating a healthy exchange of personnel between government and the private sector, and safeguarding the public interest. Major revisions of the rules in 1975 and 1980 required Permanent Secretaries to ensure that there is at least a three-month gap between resignation or retirement and taking up a new post, and obliged officials in the top three grades of the civil service to obtain Cabinet Office approval before accepting any appointments in business within two years of leaving the service. In addition, the cases of people from the top two grades, and their military equivalents, are referred to the Prime Minister's Advisory Committee on Business Appointments. Even officials outside the most senior grades may have to seek permission to take up new posts with companies with whom they have had official dealings, or if they have had access to sensitive information about a company's competitors. Under the rules, the government may impose waiting periods of up to two years before certain appointments can be undertaken, and restrictions may be imposed in some cases (for example, no direct contacts with the official's former department on a specified contract).

None the less, despite these rules, concern has been repeatedly expressed by MPs and others about the implications of post-retirement jobs. They point to the scale of these appointments, to the fact that only a tiny proportion of the thousands of applications made under the government's rules are ever rejected, to the fact

that the rules have no legal force, and to the remarkable rise in post-retirement appointments in the defence industries, where the opportunities for exchanging sensitive information are significant. Applications from Ministry of Defence officials quadrupled in the period 1979–92 and came to account for 30 per cent of all requests (Pallister and Norton-Taylor, 1992a). The former Permanent Secretary of the MoD, Sir Frank Cooper, took up a series of posts with defence contractors (including the chairmanship of United Scientific Holdings, and a directorship with Westland Helicopters) after leaving Whitehall in 1983. His lead was followed by hundreds of his former subordinates (over 300 in 1990 alone).

Commons select committees, especially the Treasury and Civil Service Committee, have investigated the 'revolving door' phenomenon on a number of occasions. In 1984, this Committee recommended a substantial tightening of the government's rules, to encompass the following:

- A ban on senior civil servants having discussions with prospective employers during the last year of service before retirement.
- A ban on senior officials taking up private-sector posts within five years of retirement or resignation.
- A strengthened role for the Advisory Committee on Business Appointments.
- Limitations on the matters for which former civil servants could assume responsibility in their new jobs.
- Withdrawal of pensions in cases where the rules were flouted.

The government responded by rejecting these proposals, on the grounds that it had no desire to restrict freedom of movement between the public and private sectors, and, in any case, there was no evidence that the existing rules were being abused (HM Treasury, 1985).

Following publication of the findings of David Pallister and Richard Norton-Taylor, the Cabinet Secretary and Head of the Home Civil Service wrote to *The Guardian*, defending the existing arrangements (Butler, 1992b). He argued that the rules worked effectively, and the national interest as well as the personal interest of the individuals concerned was well served by 'a reasonable flow of people from the public to the private sector'.

Effect of Next Steps on the policy role of civil servants

If we accept that government ministers, as a fundamental aspect of their role responsibility, have a need to offer policy leadership, and civil servants in the middle to upper reaches of the departmental hierarchy are charged with the task of offering policy advice (as well as implementing or executing policy), what conclusions are we able to draw about the effect of Next Steps in the realm of policy? Potentially, the Next Steps initiative was to have some implications for the policy-making environment within government departments. Although attention naturally centres on the policy-implementation and service-delivery aspects of Next Steps, the creation of executive agencies was meant to 'free' the core, parent departments from day-to-day administrative concerns, thus facilitating greater emphasis on policy. As Greer has commented: 'Next Steps calls for departmental headquarters' senior civil servants to employ a different set of skills. They are to become more strategic' (Greer, 1992: 227). The Fraser Report, reviewing progress with Next Steps after three years, indicated that a great deal of ground had still to be covered in this respect, and recommended that 'Once [the] initial tasks are complete and the Department has defined its role in relation to Agencies, the functions and staffing of its headquarters should be reduced' (Efficiency Unit, 1991: para. 2.14). Taken to extremes, the Next Steps initiative could have produced a basic model of the relationship between an agency and its parent department which allocated a minimal or non-existent policy advice role to the agency officials. Thus, the ministers and senior civil servants in the parent department together formulate policy, which is simply passed on to the agency for efficient, effective and economical implementation in line with the agency's stated objectives. In this light, the extant responsibilities of ministers and senior civil servants in the parent department for, respectively, policy leadership and policy advice, would remain largely unaffected by the advent of Next Steps, while the civil servants working in the agencies (even the Chief Executives and their senior management boards) would have no role responsibility for policy advice as such.

However, the Ibbs Report (Efficiency Unit, 1988), which presaged the Next Steps programme, and the Fraser Report (Efficiency Unit, 1991), which reviewed progress after three years, as well as government responses to the Treasury and Civil Service Select Committee's reports, did not set out a precise definition of the policy role to be ascribed to the agencies. Instead, while there was clearly an underlying assumption that a policy/administration dichotomy existed, the agency Framework Documents were repeatedly mentioned as the source of information on relationships between particular agencies and their departmental parents.

An analysis of the Framework Documents offers us the possibility of two types of policy role for agencies. The minimalist role, as set out above, can be dismissed as a working model. Agency Chief Executives and management boards were clearly allocated policy advice roles in relation to the particular sphere covered by the agency in question. As Davies and Willman have noted, this is simple good sense:

> it is a reasonable hypothesis that Agencies, particularly in highly specialised areas, will play a substantial, if not always an attributable, role in the formulation of policy. Indeed, it is a nonsense to exclude them, even theoretically, from this exercise. The act of target-setting is, in itself, a matter of policy and if this is to be realistic the experience of the Agency will be a decisive factor. (Davies and Willman, 1991: 33)

None the less, a distinction can be drawn between those agencies and Chief Executives who have been allocated what might be described as a 'sleeping' role in policy advice (that is, to provide ministers and senior officials in the parent department with advice as requested – see, for example, the Framework Document of the Social Security Benefits Agency), and those who have been allocated a more pro-active role in this sphere (that is, to participate fully in the parent department's policy-making machinery – see, for example, the Framework Document of the Employment Services Agency).

There seemed to be a long-term possibility of an enhancement to the policy role of senior civil servants in the parent department. As Patrick Dunleavy has noted,

> some people argue that the policy/administration dichotomy is still there, but it's no longer one between politicians and civil servants, it's between politicians and high civil servants on the one hand, and management, implementation-oriented, middle range civil servants on the other. (Dunleavy, quoted in Hennessy and Coates, 1992: 7)

Although it is likely to take the experience of a decade or more with executive agencies before it will be possible to conclude that this has happened, or will happen, in British government (and the policy role of the Employment Service Agency Chief Executive would seem to challenge Dunleavy's vision), it is one possible outcome of Next Steps.

The net effect would seem to be that Next Steps has served to emphasise, and in some cases develop, the existing policy advice role of civil servants (with the potential to do more in this regard over the longer term) while pointing to the continued difficulty in establishing clear demarcation lines between policy advice and the creation of policy.

Theories, models and reality

Modelling the policy process: part I

When considering the part played by civil servants in policy-making, it is important to grasp the complexity of this process. Numerous theoretical models of the policy process exist, and many of these are highly sophisticated. Hogwood and Gunn (1984), for example, have described the policy cycle with reference to nine interlinked stages, from 'deciding to decide' to 'policy maintenance, succession or termination'. A more concise model has been utilised by Philip Norton (1993), describing four principal stages in the process ('initiation', 'formulation', 'deliberation and approval' and 'implementation').

Taking Norton's model, for the sake of convenience, we could establish a very simplistic interpretation of the policy process, which would see policy initiated by the majority party, formulated and refined by ministers and their senior officials, deliberated upon and approved by Parliament and implemented by the civil service or another appropriate arm of the state.

In fact, it is extremely doubtful whether the policy cycle ever operated in such a mechanistic fashion, and it would certainly be quite misleading to describe it in these terms today. Apart from anything else, as Norton points out, policy proposals 'may emanate from different sources, such as individuals, pressure groups and companies' (Norton, 1993: 52). Jordan and Richardson have gone further, citing six policy-making 'arenas', occupied by the political parties, the public, Parliament, the Cabinet, the bureaucracy and pressure groups (Jordan and Richardson, 1987). They might have added an international arena, including bodies such as NATO, the United Nations and the European Union.

There are two key points to understand here. The first is that, while serving the central executive in the realm of policy formation, civil servants have a role which is far from negligible. The second is that the role of the civil service has to be located in a broader context than traditional accounts of minister–civil servant relations allow. Let us develop these points, with reference to the complex reality of the policy process.

If the kind of policy cycle mentioned above is to be dismissed as too crude and simplistic, how does the policy process actually operate, and what part is played by the civil service?

Jordan and Richardson have described the most common style of policy-making in Britain as a form of 'bureaucratic accommodation' involving the creation of consensus and agreement within the key 'policy communities'. We shall return to this in due course, but first it must be recognised, as Jordan and Richardson do, that policy is not invariably made in this way. Thus, some policies, such as those involving constitutional change, are formulated through referenda or electoral politics. The part played by the civil service here may be fairly limited. Others, including the most highly sensitive foreign and defence policies, are produced in private, within the government machine, and here the role of the civil service is likely to be greater. Finally, policies which take the form of party commitments or have a strongly ideological flavour may have been formulated in the policy-making machinery of the governing party, or through the work of special political advisers and 'think tanks', before being presented at the highest levels· of government in a largely non-negotiable form.

Officials, special political advisers and think tanks: from the Cabinet Office and Number 10 to the Adam Smith Institute

The latter point merits further comment. There have been occasions when the roles played by political advisers and external think tanks have been perceived as encroaching upon the traditional sphere of the civil service in policy advice. However, before developing this theme, we must place our comments in perspective. The role of the official machine has always been, and remains, significant. Officials operating from the Cabinet Office and from 10 Downing Street, continue to serve the very core of the central executive in an extremely important fashion.

The Cabinet Office consists of around 650–700 civil servants, mainly located in six secretariats (dealing with Home Affairs, the Economy, Europe, Science and Technology, Security and Intelligence, and Overseas and Defence Policy), each of which is headed by an Under Secretary, with the Cabinet Secretary, Sir Robin Butler, heading the entire structure. It performs a variety of functions, ranging from the preparation of agendas for meetings of the full Cabinet and Cabinet committees, briefing committee chairmen, taking minutes, circulating decisions and chasing-up their implementation across Whitehall. It has been argued (Seldon, 1990: 108–9) that some of the secretariats are more 'proactive' in framing policy agendas (the European, and the Science and Technology secretariats), while the others tend to be 'reactive' in the sense that they operate in spheres with long-established policy links within and beyond Whitehall.

Cabinet Secretaries exercise varying degrees of power and influence over government policy, depending to a very considerable extent upon the respective personalities and strengths of the Prime Ministers and Secretaries concerned, and the circumstances of the time (for example, Norman Brook wielded great power in the latter part of the Churchill administration between 1953 and 1955, due to the premier's poor health). The very nature of the job gives every Cabinet Secretary many opportunities. These include daily discussions with the PM, attendance at Cabinet meetings, the chance to advise senior members of the government on the precise timing and substance of policy decisions, acting as the Prime Minister's personal representative in advance of economic and Commonwealth summits, and operating as the Premier's principal official adviser on security and intelligence matters.

We can add to this the parts played by civil servants in the various component parts of the Prime Minister's Office. Especially worthy of note are the Principal Private Secretary and the six Private Secretaries who staff the Private Office at Number 10. Under Margaret Thatcher, one of these Private Secretaries, Charles Powell, came to have considerable influence as a key adviser in foreign affairs. The Press and Information Office has normally been headed by civil servants who are specialist Information Officers (although Clement Attlee and Harold Wilson appointed sympathetic journalists as their Press Secretaries). For virtually all of the Thatcher period the Press and Information Office was headed by Bernard Ingham, who, although a civil servant (albeit one with a background in journalism), became one of the PM's closest advisers on a range of political and presentational matters (for contrasting views of Ingham's role, see Ingham, 1991; and Harris, 1991). Under John Major, the role of the Press Secretary became less assertive (he immediately dispensed with Ingham's services, and the post was given, successively, to two more conventional Information Officers, Gus O'Donnell (1990–3) and Christopher Meyer (from January 1994)).

What can we say about the role of political advisers and external think tanks? Departmental ministers have been drawing on the services of special political advisers for some time. Until the 1970s, their numbers were fairly small, but in 1974 there was a substantial increase, with thirty-eight special advisers being appointed, partly as a consequence of the view that radical ministers needed to be buttressed against the neutralising impulses of their senior civil servants (Young, 1976; Blackstone, 1979). Although the numbers tended to fluctuate thereafter, special advisers (from the party, academia or the business world) continued to be used by Labour and Conservative ministers alike. In some cases, as with Tony Benn's advisers in the Departments of Industry and Energy between 1974 and 1979, there was considerable friction between the advisers and civil servants, but, in the main, special advisers tend to complement rather than usurp the departmental officials. Attempts to formalise and strengthen the role of special advisers, by allowing ministers to appoint continental-style *cabinets*, have never come to anything (for useful discussions of the *cabinet* concept, see Neville-Jones, 1983; and Treasury and Civil Service Committee, 1986). None the less, the evidence taken by the Treasury and Civil Service Committee in the course of its wide-ranging inquiry into the role of the civil service reveals the abiding attraction of such devices for some observers and insiders (Treasury and Civil Service Committee, 1993).

A more formidable threat to the policy role of civil servants has come from the array of think tanks and special political advisers orbiting around 10 Downing Street. It is in this realm of strategic policy advice that the civil service arguably lost some ground to outsiders, of various descriptions, particularly in the period since the late 1970s, although the balance may have been redressed somewhat during the Major premiership.

The Prime Minister's political advisers come in two forms. There are those who have an official status, as members of the Downing Street Political Office (under Thatcher and Major these were mainly fairly low-key officials seconded from Conservative Party Central Office) or the Policy Unit (which consists of civil servants and outsiders on attachment to the service). The Policy Unit is an important element of the Prime Minister's Office, and attracted a great deal of attention in the 1980s under Sir John Hoskyns, Ferdinand Mount, John Redwood and Brian Griffiths. Sarah Hogg, a professional journalist, headed John Major's Policy Unit until January 1995, when she left to be replaced by Norman Blackwell. These advisers tend to operate in close conjunction and relative harmony with the civil service. The second type of Prime Ministerial adviser operates in an individual capacity, usually covering a specific policy sphere, and may or may not enjoy formal status in Downing Street. This type was exemplified by Sir Alan Walters, the academic economist who operated as an adviser to Margaret Thatcher during two distinct periods. The second came to an end in 1989, when Walters' advice on European monetary policy came into conflict with the official Treasury line, and led to the resignation of the Chancellor of the Exchequer, Nigel Lawson. It was part of the character of the Thatcher premiership that she posed as an outsider in her own administration, had an intrinsic distrust of the great departments of state and leant heavily upon her own special advisers in economic, defence and foreign policy.

Her basic approach was to seek out policy advice which was of an avowedly ideological nature. Thus, in 1983 she abolished the Central Policy Review Staff, the government's own think tank, within which seconded civil servants and outsiders had worked to offer strategic policy advice to the Cabinet as a whole. Instead, she preferred to exploit her free access to three external think tanks (the Centre for Policy Studies, the Adam Smith Institute and the Institute of Economic Affairs), each of which dealt in the currency of New Right political philosophy.

The period after 1990, with a new presence in Number 10, witnessed less reliance by the Prime Minister upon special policy advisers of the Walters type, and a marked demotion of the external think tanks (O'Hagan, 1991; White, 1993). It should be remembered that, even at the height of their influence, political advisers and think tanks rarely played decisive roles in the creation of policy, and always operated in the shadow and continuing power of the Downing Street and Cabinet Office machines.

Modelling the policy process: part 2

Earlier, reference was made to the argument of Jordan and Richardson that the most common style of policy-making in Britain is a form of 'bureaucratic accommodation'. Let us return to this.

While it is important to recognise that there is much co-ordination across Whitehall, and to understand that what occurs in the policy sphere of one department is usually of interest and relevance to others, it is also clear that departments operate in relatively distinct fiefdoms. Departmental ministers and civil servants jealously guard their policy 'territory' against encroachment by rivals. Furthermore, there exists an interdependence between, on the one hand, a department of state, and on the other, the client groups operating in its broad policy field. While making allowance for the fact that departments and their associated pressure and interest groups can come into conflict, Jordan and Richardson argue,

> Viewing central government as essentially pluralistic in nature, that is, a collection of separate policy sectors reflected in departmental boundaries, leads naturally to . . . clientistic relationships . . . in which the essential nature of the relationship between departments and groups is negotiative. (Jordan and Richardson, 1987: 170)

The implications of this for civil servants are significant. When helping their ministers to design policies, senior officials are likely to spend a considerable amount of time as participants in particular policy communities, liaising, consulting and negotiating with the key pressure and interest groups. As a general rule, civil servants prefer to over-consult rather than under-consult the major interests in their policy community (Grant, 1989: 60–1). While the views and preferences of the organised interests are not invariably accepted by departments, there is a predisposition towards establishing consensus and agreement, especially with the major groups.

In every corner of Whitehall, the interaction between officials and organised interests forms a key element of the policy-making process. Thus, for example, agricultural policy cannot be properly understood without taking account of the relationship between MAFF officials and the National Farmers' Union. Similarly in the health policy community, the links between the Department of Health and the Royal Colleges are highly significant, as are those between the DTI, trade associations and individual companies in the trade policy community.

In this chapter we have examined a range of key issues surrounding the high policy advice role of the civil service. We shall return to consider further aspects of the minister–civil servant relationship in the context of our discussions of accountability and official secrecy, in later chapters. However, at this stage, it would be logical and appropriate for us to focus on the role of the civil service in policy implementation.

5

IMPLEMENTING PUBLIC POLICY
A service of quality?

We have seen that the roles of civil servants can be categorised as involving the provision of policy advice to ministers, departmental or agency management, and the delivery, administration or implementation of policy. Our primary concern in this chapter is with the latter role. The implementation of public policy by the civil service has been affected to a degree by the creation of the Next Steps executive agencies, and the concomitant emphasis on 'quality' of service, epitomised by the Citizen's Charter and associated devices.

Policy implementation is a deceptively complex concept. In order to approach a full understanding of the implications of recent structural changes for the implementation of public policy by the civil service, it is important for us to give the concept some further consideration.

Policy implementation

Changing the face of policy implementation

Traditionally, the implementation of policy by the British civil service was characterised by the following:

- A belief that 'policy' and 'administration' could be disaggregated: the former being very much the preserve of ministers, with a minor, secondary role allotted to senior civil servants as policy advisers, and the latter (encompassing the implementation of policy) being the sphere of middle- and low-ranking officials.
- The use of highly centralised organisational structures, tightly integrated with Whitehall departments or their regional outposts.
- Little or no scope for variety and flexibility in service provision.
- Remoteness, in terms of the 'arm's-length' relationship between the departmental officials delivering the service and the 'clients' on the receiving end.
- The existence of, at best, very general mechanisms for the purpose of checking on the quality and standard of service being delivered.

Keith Dowding has encapsulated the more extreme implications of this traditional approach to implementation:

> The classic defence of straightforward hierarchical organization within a public bureaucracy involves the idea that civil servants are implementors who methodically apply rules to particular cases 'read off' from their rule book. They have clearly demarcated spheres of competence and can act as impersonal cyphers for their political masters' policies. (Dowding, 1993: 239)

Notwithstanding all this, modern theories of public policy-making ascribe a key role to implementation in the context of the policy process. Thus, for example, as mentioned in the previous chapter, Hogwood and Gunn analyse the process with reference to nine stages, from 'deciding to decide (issue search or agenda setting)' to 'policy maintenance, succession or termination' (Hogwood and Gunn, 1984: *passim*). The seventh stage is policy implementation, but this should not be viewed as something totally distinct from other stages. On the contrary;

> there is no sharp divide between (a) formulating a policy and (b) implementing that policy. What happens at the so-called 'implementation' stage will influence the actual policy outcome. Conversely, the probability of a successful outcome (which we define . . . as that outcome desired by the initiators of the policy) will be increased if

> thought has been given at the policy design stage to potential problems of implementation. (Hogwood and Gunn, 1984: 198)

Thus, it can be argued that there are very close links between the implementation of any given policy and the policy-making process. At the very least, this implies something less than a rigid differentiation between matters of 'policy' on the one hand, and matters of 'administration' on the other: shades of grey rather than a black-and-white distinction.

The extent to which the Next Steps initiative took this on board is open to question (see Chapter 4). As we have seen, there are some senses in which Next Steps was predicated upon a fairly rigid policy/administration divide, and, as we shall see in Chapter 6, this contributed to problems in relation to accountability.

None the less, the initiative did herald the advent of a new approach to policy implementation, at least in the rather limited sense that the basic structures for implementation were to be overhauled. The civil service would implement policy via the new executive agencies, which would be linked to, but at the same time distinct from, their parent departments of state. The executive agencies would be given considerable freedom to develop variety and flexibility in service provision. They would be much more 'customer-friendly' than the old offshoots of centralised government departments. The executive agencies would also be required to develop mechanisms for monitoring the standards of service being delivered, and for securing 'quality' in service provision. Part of the drive for the improvement of standards and quality would come from within the framework of the Next Steps initiative itself, and part from other, associated government initiatives, as we shall see.

In practice, the executive agencies which could be categorised as 'Mainstream' or 'Regulatory and other Statutory agencies' (Efficiency Unit, 1991: Annex A) would be most involved in the implementation of departmental policy. Agencies in other categories, including those providing internal specialist services to their departments or other agencies, would be less obviously concerned with policy implementation and external service delivery.

The theory of 'perfect implementation'

Drawing upon, and developing the ideas of Hood (1976), Hogwood and Gunn set out the preconditions for 'perfect implementation'

(Hogwood and Gunn, 1984: Chapter 11), while emphasising that this is impossible to achieve in practice. It is worthwhile recounting these preconditions, in order to draw attention to the extent to which Next Steps sought (consciously or otherwise) to enhance implementation. Thus, according to Hogwood and Gunn, the preconditions for 'perfect implementation' are as follows:

- The circumstances external to the implementing agency do not impose crippling constraints: this refers to a whole range of possible obstacles to implementation, including physical and political factors. Next Steps agencies were not, and could not be, specifically designed to be exempt from these types of constraints.

- Adequate time and sufficient resources are made available to the programme to be implemented. Next Steps agencies were not, and could not be, specifically designed to be exempt from these limitations.

- The required combination of resources is actually available. Next Steps agencies were not, and could not be, specifically designed to be exempt from these limitations.

- The policy to be implemented is based upon a valid theory of cause and effect: this refers to the creation of 'bad' policies, which cannot be properly implemented simply because they are based upon a poor understanding of the problem being addressed and the extent to which it can be resolved. It might be argued that the example of the Child Support Agency and the implementation of the policy designed to make 'absent fathers' pay more money towards the upkeep of their children provides us with a case study in this category. Of course, this raises the issue of the proper role of agencies in the policy-making process. Arguably, the allocation of a pro-active as opposed to a 'sleeping' role in the provision of policy advice to ministers by agencies would result in fewer problems at the implementation stage. However, as we saw in Chapter 4, there are certainly significant differences in the policy roles ascribed to different Next Steps agencies.

- The relationship between cause and effect is direct and there are few, if any, intervening links: this refers to the need to avoid over-complex policy programmes delivered via extended causal chains. In fact, those Next Steps agencies which have responsibility for delivering a myriad of interlinked services (such as the Social Security Benefits Agency) face precisely this sort of problem.

- Dependency relationships are minimal: this refers to the need for a single implementing agency wherever possible. While some Next Steps agencies effectively enjoy monopoly status in the sense that they are the sole or dominant bodies in their field, many are required to liaise with a whole range of other participating bodies, including local authorities and other central government agencies.

- There is understanding of, and agreement on, objectives. Here, there is some evidence that the creation of the Next Steps agencies involved an explicit attempt to overcome a perceived weakness in the traditional system of policy implementation. The agency Framework Documents contain clear statements of objectives agreed between the agencies and the parent departments. However, some of these are rather imprecise and highly generalised.

- Tasks are fully specified in correct sequence: this involves the detailed delineation of objectives, set out in a logical sequence. Next Steps agencies would, in theory, facilitate and enhance this process.

- There is perfect communication and co-ordination. While it was to be hoped that the creation of the Next Steps agencies would lead to the establishment of clearer lines of communication and more coherent systems of co-ordination (and, indeed, the organisational structures of the agencies were designed partly with this objective in mind), the achievement of perfection in this sphere is unattainable.

- Those in authority can demand and obtain perfect compliance. Perfect implementation can be guaranteed if, *inter alia*, superiors can command total and immediate compliance from their subordinates within the organisation. Even if this was desirable (and, clearly it is not – there may be circumstances in any organ-isation where it is necessary and appropriate for subordinates to question and delay the implementation of orders passed down to them) the Next Steps agencies were not designed to accom-modate such a scenario.

Closely associated with the implementation of policy *per se* is the question of service quality. To state that the civil service has re-sponsibility for implementing a specific public policy takes us only so far: the extent to which officials show a concern for matters of quality while implementing the policy requires closer examination.

The 'quality' agenda

The meaning of quality

The concept of quality has come to feature prominently in the language of public service delivery and implementation during the 1990s. As with many of the other managerial initiatives which have been introduced in the civil service, the growing concern for quality had its origins in private-sector management. In this sense, we are witnessing another attempt to transplant an aspect of American business philosophy into the culture of the British civil service (and beyond, throughout the public sector as a whole).

The genesis of quality management in private-sector organisa-tions is difficult to pinpoint with accuracy. It can certainly be traced back to some US business corporations in the 1920s, although argua-bly the most significant developments in the application of the con-cept took place in both the United States and Japan from the 1950s onwards. A particular focus upon quality in relation to securing excellence in the delivery of 'outputs' was developed in the writings of prominent American analysts in the 1980s (Peters and Waterman, 1982; Peters and Austin, 1985; Peters, 1987).

How was it that a deeply rooted concept which was deemed appropriate in the context of process and manufacturing indus-tries, where its purpose was primarily to fine-tune production pro-cesses, maintain the suitability of products and secure competitive advantages, came to be applied in the public sector? Peter Hinton offers an explanation:

> At first sight, it might appear that a private sector quality approach
> is not directly suited to public service organizations. . . . However, it
> is the efficiency savings and customer care aspects of a quality pro-
> gramme which are attractive to service organizations. Unit cost
> measurements may be inadequately precise and market research of
> customer requirements may be less developed, but this does not
> restrict the application of a quality approach. (Hinton, 1993: 64)

In time, the messages contained in the private-sector business
manuals came to be adapted, and tailored to the needs of the
public sector. However, it should be noted that the more populist,
high-profile approaches, epitomised by Osborne and Gaebler's *Reinventing Government*, have been criticised on the grounds that
they lack academic rigour (Jordan, 1994; Rhodes, 1994).

To argue that the concept of quality can be applied in the context of service delivery and policy implementation leaves us some-
where short of an understanding of the concept itself. What does
'quality' mean in this context, what are the difficulties associated
with its measurement and which mechanisms and strategies have
been adopted in order to enhance the quality of service delivered
by officials?

If we are to judge by the statements offered in many of the
managerialist tomes, 'quality' is a rather elusive concept, the defi-
nitions of which tend to be characterised by vagueness and gener-
alisation. Thus, we end up with 'quality assurance checklists' which
tend to contain, *inter alia*, injunctions to do the following:

- Establish clear targets and objectives.
- Set acceptable standards of service, and facilitate regular improvements in these.
- Identify the aspects of a service which are of greatest significance to customers and their needs (for example, no long
  waiting periods).
- Assess problems or failings which arise in relation to these
  needs (for example, serious delays, long queues for service).
- Respond to customer needs and expectations by introducing
  improvements (for example, employing more staff at key service delivery desks during busy periods, or introducing more
  realistic appointment systems).
- Show a consistent concern for openness and accessibility.
- Secure speedy redress of legitimate grievances.

- Introduce systems for continuously monitoring all of the above.

As Christopher Pollitt has argued, this type of approach places great emphasis on 'the need for explicit, public indicators of standards. It also emphasizes the central importance of service user (or 'consumer') judgements of the appropriateness and effectiveness of services' (Pollitt, 1990: 437). Some analysts (Pollitt among them) probe beneath the surface of the quality assurance checklists, however, and offer us more revealing insights into the meaning and application of quality. Kieron Walsh, for example, differentiates between two basic elements of quality. The first is centred on the 'product' itself (which may be a particular service), and sees quality as a measure of the extent to which the 'product' conforms to its specification. Thus, the customers, consumers or clients of the service may have the right to expect redress or remedies if the quality of service provided falls short of the published objectives. Walsh's second element concerns the extent to which the 'product' is fit for the purpose for which it is intended: this may not always be the case, even if a service is delivered in line with stated objectives! (Walsh, 1991: 503–4).

However, while justifying the need for attention to be given to matters of quality in the delivery of public services, Walsh, and other commentators (Walsh, 1991: 506; Bowen and Schneider, 1988; Pollitt, 1990) point to the inherent difficulties in measuring quality in this sphere.

Firstly, public services are less tangible than the material products of commercial organisations, and this makes them difficult to test and measure. Inevitably, analytical objectivity is more difficult to secure, and the risks of subjective, value-judgements are more serious.

Secondly, services are 'consumed' as they are 'produced', and this makes it very difficult to establish procedures for filtering out sub-standard 'products'. This implies the need for quality control systems to operate concurrently with the delivery of the services (rather than separately, as is the case in the commercial world, where 'bad products' can be filtered out before they reach the customers).

Thirdly, in many cases the 'producer' of the service (for example, the civil servant delivering social security benefits across the counter of a Benefits Agency office) is effectively part of the 'product', because a personal relationship with the 'customer' is involved.

Fourthly, the 'customer' is an inherent element of the 'production' of services. While manufactured goods exist whether or not the customers make use of them, many public services can only be 'produced' when the recipients (those receiving social security benefits, for example) play their part in the process.

Finally, the role of the customer in quality assurance systems is problematic: professionals charged with the delivery of services are often reluctant to face up to the implications of 'quality' judgements being made by those receiving the services.

For Walsh, the difficulties associated with measuring quality in public services, are accentuated by the fact that 'services are fundamentally different from manufactured goods, and public services even more so ... [making] the judgement of quality a potentially difficult and contested exercise' (Walsh, 1991: 508).

Given the conceptual and definitional problems associated with quality, what approach has been taken in setting the quality agenda within the civil service?

Next Steps and quality

The quality of service provision and policy implementation by Next Steps executive agencies is monitored through the use of specified targets and performance indicators.

Although the Financial Management Initiative had given a spur towards the development of performance indicators in the civil service, the old departmental structures and the absence of financial and managerial incentives ensured that these devices were used only in a rather superficial fashion (Carter and Greer, 1993: 407, 415). The Next Steps initiative was to give performance targets, standards of service and performance indicators a much higher profile by linking them to the strategic objectives of the executive agencies and raising the issue of resource implications.

The choice of targets and performance indicators was for individual ministers to agree with their agency Chief Executives, although the government eventually produced a guide (HM Treasury, 1992b) when it became clear that some agencies were making considerably more progress in this respect than others, and some

Table 5.1 Key performance targets in three Executive agencies, 1993–4

Companies House

- To make all statutory documents available for public inspection within five working days of receipt.
- To satisfy all requests for searches within two hours.
- To achieve a compliance rate of 86% by end-June 1993, increasing to 90% by end-June 1994 for companies filing accounts and annual returns.
- To reduce real unit costs by an average of 2% a year.
- To achieve a 6% average annual rate of return based on the Agency's operating surplus expressed as a percentage of average net assets employed at current values.
- To reply within ten working days to letters from MPs delegated to the Chief Executive for reply.

Employment Service

- 1.47 million job placings of unemployed people of whom:
    27% will be long-term claimants
    3% will be people with disabilities
    35% will be people in inner cities.
- 65% of starts on Training for Work to be from referrals by the Employment Service.
- 87% of clients due an advisory interview to receive one, assuming 9.35–9.45 million interviews are due.
- 30% of unemployed clients due a 12-month advisory interview to start on a Jobplan workshop.
- To despatch 87% of first payments on the day that benefit entitlement is established (this figure will rise to 90% in the last quarter of the year).
- The accuracy of the total value of unemployment benefit paid to be at least 96.5%.
- 9% of initial claim enquiries not to be pursued as new claims.
- 63,000 claims to be withdrawn following investigation by Employment Service inspectors.
- To achieve £21.2 million in efficiency savings.

Social Security Benefits Agency

- To clear Social Fund Crisis Loan applications on the day the need arises.
- To clear 65% of Social Fund Community Care grant applications in 7 days and 95% in 20 days.
- To clear 71% of Income Support Claims within 5 days and 90% within 13 days.
- To clear 65% of Sickness and Invalidity Benefit Claims within 10 days and 95% within 30 days.
- To clear 67% of claims to Child Benefit within 10 days and 95% within 20 days.
- To clear 60% of claims to Family Credit within 13 days and 95% within 42 days.

continued

- To clear 65% of claims to Disability Living Allowance within 30 days and 85% within 55 days.
- To clear 65% of claims to Disability Working Allowance within 5 days.
- To pay the correct amount of Income Support in 92% of claims.
- To pay the correct amount of Incapacity Benefits in 96.5% of claims.
- To pay the correct amount of Family Credit in 92% of claims.
- To pay the correct amount of Disability Living Allowance in 96% of claims.
- To pay the correct amount of Disability Working Allowance in 95% of cases.
- 85% of customers to regard the service they receive from the Agency as satisfactory or better.
- £219 million of Social Fund expenditure to be covered by loan recoveries.
- £557 million saved through the detection and prevention of fraud.
- £54 million of benefit overpayments to be recovered.
- To manage the Agency's resources to deliver its Business Plan within the gross budget allocation.
- To achieve new efficiency savings worth at least £44.6 million.
- To keep the net cash limited provision for the discretionary Social Fund budget approved by Parliament.

Source: Chancellor of the Duchy of Lancaster (1993).

of the targets had been criticised for their lack of clarity (Treasury and Civil Service Committee, 1991a: paras 63 and 64). As Greer has pointed out, the whole process of devising performance measures and indicators became highly politicised and

> involved lengthy negotiations between central departments and agencies. The negotiations inevitably involved balancing the Treasury's requirement for greater efficiency savings with the Office of the Minister for the Civil Service's requirement to make Next Steps look a success by not making targets too challenging. (Greer, 1994: 74)

There are considerable variations in the numbers and types of targets and indicators established by different agencies, but these fall into four broad categories:

- Quality.
- Financial.
- Efficiency.
- Throughput.

Examples of the key performance targets set by three agencies for 1993–4 are given in Table 5.1.

At first, agencies were relatively slow to develop the quality of service targets and performance indicators, but by 1992 independent observers could detect increased use of devices such as market surveys and client polls (Price Waterhouse, 1992: 8). During the period between 1991 and 1993 the total number of quality targets established significantly outstripped the numbers of targets in the other categories (Prime Minister, 1991; Chancellor of the Duchy of Lancaster, 1992; 1993). None the less, even by 1993, some five years into the Next Steps initiative, ten agencies (some of which had been in existence for a number of years) were failing to set quality targets spanning one year (although some had set more general quality targets covering more than one year). The concern expressed by the Treasury and Civil Service Select Committee in 1991 seemed to retain its validity:

> examination of the targets set for the agencies shows that many of them do not have targets in all . . . areas.
>
> While the choice of targets must be for the responsible Minister . . . we see no reason why it should not be obligatory for those targets to cover each of the key areas: financial performance, quality of service and efficiency. (Treasury and Civil Service Committee, 1991a: paras 64, 65)

There is a need to retain a healthy scepticism regarding some of the quality targets. For example, while two executive agencies may claim to have achieved quality targets, in one case this might mean that there has been an increase in the percentage of customers or clients who are satisfied with the standard of service being provided, while in the other the objective may have been achieved simply through completing a 'customer survey' by a given date!

While bearing this point in mind, we can see from Table 5.2 that the percentage of quality targets achieved across the range of

Table 5.2 Quality targets achieved, 1990–3

Year	Quality targets set	Numbers achieved	% Achieved
1990–1	53	37	69.8
1991–2	166	131	78.9
1992–3	235	190	80.9

Sources: Prime Minister (1991), Chancellor of the Duchy of Lancaster (1992, 1993).

executive agencies increased over the first three years for which cumulative statistics were available, from 69.8 per cent in 1990–1, to 80.9 per cent in 1992–3.

The Citizen's Charter and quality

The Citizen's Charter was launched by Prime Minister John Major in July 1991, amidst considerable publicity. The Charter's general purpose, as summarised by the Prime Minister, was broad and wide-ranging: 'To make public services answer better to the wishes of their users, and to raise their quality overall' (Citizen's Charter, 1991: 2). The White Paper which set out the Charter's aims allocated a significant, albeit rather vague and indeterminate, place to the theme of quality. The Charter was heralded as 'a sustained new programme' for improving the quality of public services (Citizen's Charter, 1991: 4).

The combined objectives of securing qualitative improvements in service management and enhancing the means for securing redress of consumers' grievances were to permeate the entire system of public administration (the National Health Service and local government, as well as central government departments and the executive agencies). These objectives were themes which ran through the basic 'Principles of Public Service' delineated in the Charter:

- Publication of standards and performance results against set targets.
- Informativeness, openness and accessibility in the provision of services.
- Customer choice and consultation.
- Courteous and efficient customer service.
- Commitment to value for money.
- Well-publicised and readily available complaints and redress procedures.

A Citizen's Charter Unit was established alongside the extant Efficiency Unit and Next Steps Unit within the Cabinet Office, and these came under the jurisdiction of the Chancellor of the Duchy of Lancaster (William Waldegrave until July 1994, David Hunt thereafter) and his new Office of Public Service and Science. In addition, each government department was required to nominate an official (or, in some cases, a team) to oversee the development and implementation of Charter initiatives. Within a few months, a plethora of 'mini-Charters' had been published, often in varied forms for England, Scotland, Wales and Northern Ireland, covering, *inter alia*, Benefits Agency customers, people using the courts, job seekers, patients, parents, rail passengers and taxpayers. By 1994, there were thirty-eight 'mini-Charters' covering most areas of public administration (Citizen's Charter, 1994: 1).

In Chapter 6 consideration is given to the part played by the Charter in enhancing accountability. Here, our main concern is to note that the Charter's stress on quality would have implications for that part of the civil service charged with the task of implementing policy through the medium of government agencies.

The Next Steps initiative was already three years old when the Charter arrived on the scene, but the executive agencies were required to build the Charter into their operations and ethos. One analyst has pointed out that the Citizen's Charter and the Next Steps programme have become 'enmeshed' (Lewis, 1993: 316).

Thus, although the agencies in operation by 1991 had established their initial performance targets and indicators, these were now effectively subsumed within the Citizen's Charter, and were paraded by agency Chief Executives as their response to the new initiative. This was possible due to the fact that

> The Citizen's Charter makes no mention of how public organizations are meant to pursue quality management. In the spirit of the 'hands-off' management of the Next Steps initiative, agencies have . . . been allowed to develop their own approaches to quality management. (Clifford, 1993: 6)

None the less, the two agencies with the most significant role in service delivery developed their own tailored responses to the Citizen's Charter.

The Social Security Benefits Agency's Customer Charter was first published in January 1992, and a second, revised version was published in December 1993. These documents collated the agency's national performance targets and required each of the 159 districts to display local targets and standards. In September 1993, the Agency initiated moves towards the ultimate introduction of a 'one-stop' service, with even the most complex customer needs being handled by individual agency officials at single integrated counters. The first step in this direction was to ensure that, by July 1994, customers only had to go to one place to secure service. Additionally, the Benefits Agency Charter set out complaints procedures and customers' appeal and compensation rights. The material surroundings of Benefit Offices were improved through a programme of modernisation and refurbishment, and more flexible opening hours were introduced in some offices. As a means of monitoring customer satisfaction with its service provision, the Benefits Agency commissioned a national polling organisation to conduct its customer surveys.

Customer care programmes of various descriptions had been introduced by the old Employment Group before the advent of the new executive agency. The Employment Service Agency took this process a stage further when it published a Jobseeker's Charter in December 1991 setting out the agency's role in administering the unemployment benefits system, and helping people get back to work. This Charter was updated in May and September 1993, and a completely revised Jobseeker's Charter was scheduled for publication in the spring of 1994. Again, a combination of national and local standards were published (local offices were under an obligation to match or better the national standards, and, from 1994, Jobcentres were required to display comparative information on the performance of neighbouring offices). Jobcentres and Unemployment Benefit Offices were gradually being integrated, in order to offer a 'one-stop' service by 1996: two-thirds of local offices had been integrated by the early part of 1994. A further dimension of this was the move to introduce a system whereby clients would normally see the same adviser each time they have an interview (this agency differentiates between 'clients', who are 'job seekers', and 'customers', who are 'job changers' or 'employers'). Local managers were given powers to extend and vary the opening times of Jobcentres and integrated Employment Service Jobcentres. Once again, customer ('client') satisfaction surveys figured as attempts to monitor the impact of the quality initiatives.

An integral part of the Citizen's Charter initiative was the Charter Mark award scheme. This represented an attempt, on the part of the government, to recognise and reward excellence in delivering services, within the terms of the Citizen's Charter. In 1992, the first year of the scheme, 36 Charter Marks were awarded, and a further 93 were awarded in 1993 (Citizen's Charter, 1994: 74–5). The awards are held for three years, after which winners must re-apply, providing evidence of how their service provision has further improved. In the meantime, Charter Marks can be taken away if standards fall.

The extent to which this type of approach can lead to a genuine improvement in the quality of service delivered is the subject of some debate. In a very general sense, as John Mayne points out, there has been an emphasis on a new type of service provision:

> The Citizen's Charter establishes the imperative for public sector organisations . . . to serve their customers, that is to say, the specific set of people who use the particular service in question. This represents a significant move away from public sector organisations serving the public interest as a whole (through service to a minister in the case of central government) and themselves being the judges of what the public interest is. (Mayne, 1993: 330)

However, sceptics (and even those, who, like Norman Lewis, are prepared to offer 'two cheers' for the initiative) point to the failure of agencies to devise performance measures for some of their objectives, the tendency on the part of some organisations to set rather low performance targets as a means of achieving high success rates, and the government's determination to divorce the question of resources from that of quality. While it cannot be denied that some improvements in the quality of service can be achieved without a massive injection of public funds, it is obvious that there are some clear connections to be made between the level of funding and service quality.

Far from being seen as a means of injecting cash into public services, however, the Citizen's Charter came to be used by the government to spearhead a potential means of cutting costs. Thus, the Charter was not simply about making public services respond better to the needs and wishes of their customers, it was also 'about finding more effective and efficient ways of delivering those services. This inevitably means change in how services are run and organised' (Citizen's Charter, 1992: 1). In particular, fundamental questions were to be asked about the extent to which government needed to continue to carry out even those activities for which it remained ultimately responsible. This was the basic thinking behind the advent of market testing, the main thrust of which was examined in Chapter 3. The Competing for Quality programme (White Paper, 1991) was a key element of the Citizen's Charter, and the government was keen to claim credit for perceived quality improvements resulting from the market-testing process.

> Whether external or in-house teams win the work, there is a chance to focus on customer needs, to introduce new flexibilities, to set and raise standards and to reduce costs. Departments have reported that in a third of reviews, they expect quality to improve. In virtually every other case, quality will be maintained at lower cost. Standards are being specified in contracts and delivery is being monitored. (Citizen's Charter, 1994: 94)

Examples cited by the government (Citizen's Charter, 1994: 94) of quality improvements achieved by market testing included the following:

- HMSO: a successful in-house bid proposed leasing a modern warehouse with access to major distribution routes. The resultant quality improvements included an increased product range and better speed and quality of service.
- Employment Department estates maintenance: contracted out to 'professional facilities management companies' resulting in a rationalisation of previously dispersed activities, improved quality of output and value for money.

However, the association of market mechanisms with the Citizen's Charter has raised some important questions about the true purpose and function of the initiative. As we noted in Chapter 3, market testing aroused the suspicion and ire of some agency Chief Executives who might have been content to pursue their performance improvements under the broad umbrella of the Citizen's Charter, but resented the imposition of compulsory competitive tendering by another name.

Beyond this, and with more general reference to the advent of a quality agenda in the civil service, the introduction of surrogate markets in the delivery of services (surrogate, because, in the absence of true markets involving the exchange of money for services rendered, the supplier/customer relationship can only imitate that of the genuine market) is problematic. As Harrow and Talbot note, the wide range of mechanisms for improving service delivery can be seen, in part, as a reflection of the elusive nature of quality in the public sector (Harrow and Talbot, 1993).

As this chapter has shown, it is impossible to give a definitive answer to the question: has there been a qualitative improvement in the implementation of public policy by the civil service? We have been able to outline the growing concern for quality in this sphere, and we have noted the expanding use of measures and indicators designed to evaluate the quality of public service. The debates about the relative importance of managerial improvements and the funding of services in enhancing quality rage on.

If the cumulative effect of the new public management has been to bring about a closer alignment between private- and public-sector management processes and techniques, what has become of the concept of accountability, traditionally cited as one of the distinguishing characteristics of governmental organisations? The next chapter adopts a wide-ranging approach to the issues of accountability and redress of grievances.

6

ACCOUNTABILITY AND REDRESS OF GRIEVANCES

Accountability is one of the key precepts of public administration and serves, in part, to differentiate it from private business and management. It is a deceptively simple proposition that civil servants should be held properly accountable for the work they do, and that there should be adequate mechanisms for citizens, clients or customers of the public services to secure redress of grievances caused by official acts (or failure to act).

Complications arise when we begin to pose questions such as the following:

Accountable for what?
Accountable to whom?
How can grievances be redressed?
What forms might redress take?

This chapter will seek to offer some clues about possible answers to these, and other questions.

Benchmarks of accountability

As we have already seen, civil servants carry out an extremely wide range of tasks and functions. They deal directly with members of the public who are claiming unemployment and other state benefits, they process applications for driving licences, they manage fisheries protection regimes, they conduct scientific and technical research, they write briefings for government ministers; the list could go on and on. If we stand back from the sheer multiplicity of civil service functions, it could be argued, along the lines suggested in Chapter 2, that three very general types of role emerge.

The first is concerned with providing policy advice for ministers, and forms the primary responsibility of the most senior Whitehall officials. This involves giving verbal and written briefings to departmental ministers which set out the legal, technical and political implications of policy options, and helping ministers mould and defend their policies in the light of parliamentary and other forms of scrutiny.

The second role may overlap with the first, and involves managing a department of state, an executive agency, or a part thereof. Management of budgets, personnel and other resources is a responsibility of civil servants up and down the departmental and agency hierarchies, from the Permanent Secretaries and agency Chief Executives to the Higher Executive Officers and others who must manage local outposts of the government empire.

Finally, there is the service delivery, policy execution or policy implementation role, which is the main working activity of the great majority of civil servants, and the improvement of which was the prime motivation behind the establishment of the Next Steps agencies.

Thus, in the most broad terms, we can say that civil servants are accountable for policy advice, departmental and agency management and policy implementation.

Officials are accountable for the efficient, effective and economical discharge of these responsibilities to their civil service line managers (up to, and including the Permanent Secretary of the department, and beyond, to the Head of the Civil Service), their ministers, in certain strictly regulated circumstances to Parliament, and in only the most remote (and constitutionally unacknowledged) circumstances, to the public.

In order to make sense of the various strands of civil service accountability, we shall look in turn at internal and then external mechanisms, before examining the controversies surrounding the impact of Next Steps in this context. Let us first focus our attention on the internal manifestation of accountability: to civil service line managers and to ministers.

Internal accountability

If we were to judge the efficacy of systems of accountability solely in terms of the number of mechanisms available, we would have to conclude that the 1980s and early 1990s witnessed a clear improvement in the accountability of civil servants to their official and ministerial superiors. As the managerialist wave of this era swept over Whitehall and the regional outposts of the civil service, the Rayner scrutinies, management information systems and the Financial Management Initiative brought in their wake a myriad of new techniques and procedures, designed in part to enhance accountability (Metcalf and Richards, 1990).

Devolved responsibility for budgets, resources and personnel management, and the advent of performance targets and reviews were primarily geared towards the achievement of greater economy, efficiency and effectiveness, but these initiatives would facilitate greater accountability for departmental management and, by implication, for the implementation of policy.

According to this model, a vital prerequisite of enhanced internal accountability was a clearer definition of specific civil service roles and responsibilities. For example, in order to establish clear lines of internal financial accountability, 'cost-centres' and budget holders had to be identified at middle and low levels of the departmental hierarchy. The cost-centre managers or budget holders were obliged to clarify their activities and the costs of carrying these out, assume responsibility for the delegated budget and account for the management of this in due course to civil service line managers and, ultimately, ministers.

For this and similar managerial initiatives to take root throughout the civil service would be the task of years, perhaps decades. None the less, it is possible to offer the tentative conclusion that the systems of internal accountability, especially for financial management, were gradually being enhanced by the advent of the new managerialism. The managerial reforms also had implications for the external accountability of civil servants,

however, and there would be much more controversy about the
results in this sphere.

External accountability

In simple terms, we might consider the possibility that civil servants could be externally accountable (i.e. accountable to sources
beyond their departmental ministers and official superiors) to Parliament, or beyond, to the public. However, the proposition that
civil servants can be accountable to such external sources is extremely problematic. The primacy of the doctrine of individual
ministerial responsibility ensures that as far as the British constitution is concerned, the accountability of civil servants begins and
ends with the internal sources, with the sole exception of the Accounting Officer (normally the Permanent Secretary of the department) who is directly accountable to Parliament in the form of the
Public Accounts Committee of the House of Commons.

The aftermath of the Sarah Tisdall and Clive Ponting cases in
1984–5 (Pyper, 1985; Ponting, 1986), as well as that of Colette
Bowe during the Westland affair in 1986 (Linklater and Leigh,
1986; Madgwick and Woodhouse, 1989), together with the publication of the Armstrong Memorandum (for more detail on all of
these, see Chapter 7) served to emphasise the very limited nature
of civil service accountability in strict constitutional terms.

It could be argued, however, that there have been some rather
important developments in this sphere in the period since the
1960s. In particular, we might wish to draw a distinction between
the *de jure* non-accountability of civil servants to Parliament (with
the exception of the aforementioned link between Accounting
Officers and the Public Accounts Committee) and an emerging *de
facto* accountability, exemplified by the work of House of Commons select committees and the Parliamentary Commissioner for
Administration (Pyper, 1987a). In this light, we could say that
external accountability of civil servants to Parliament has improved, although there is clearly considerable scope for further
improvement.

Genuine public accountability and direct redress of citizens'
grievances remains embryonic at best, but it would be wrong to say
that there have been no developments in this field. Let us examine

these points in more detail, starting with the question of parliamentary accountability.

Parliament

The primary function of most parliamentary mechanisms of accountability is to enable MPs to examine ministers on the creation, management and implementation of government policy. Some of the mechanisms touch civil servants more directly than others, but all impinge upon the working routine of a wide range of officials.

While those studying the techniques of parliamentary scrutiny tend to concentrate on formal mechanisms and devices, informal contacts between MPs and ministers should not be ignored. Indeed, there is some evidence to support the view that personal correspondence between MPs seeking redress of constituents' grievances and departmental ministers increased remarkably in the period since 1945 (Marsh, 1985). Furthermore, it is quite clear that personal letters addressed by MPs to ministers are treated very seriously indeed within government departments (Norton, 1981). An MP's letter will elicit much more specific, detailed information than would be the case if the matter had simply been raised on the floor of the House. These missives go straight to an Assistant Secretary, who will initiate a high-priority investigation of the subject, thereby bringing officials further down the departmental chain of command to account for their actions in the realm of departmental management and policy implementation. The final reply, which may be fairly voluminous, is placed on the minister's desk for signing. This process plays a part in bringing about ministerial accountability to Parliament, but also facilitates improved accountability of civil servants to their political and administrative superiors and, albeit indirectly, to Parliament.

Parliamentary Questions (PQs) (Chester, 1981; Franklin and Norton, 1993) may be placed for oral or written answer. Departmental ministers answer PQs orally in a rota which is designed to facilitate more regular questioning of those ministers whose departments attract most questions. While the initial oral PQ is notified to the minister in advance, supplementary questions are not. Written PQs tend to seek more detailed information, often of a statistical type. Departmental ministers appear at the despatch box to answer oral PQs and are named as the respondents to the questions for written answer, but the information contained in each type of answer is compiled by civil servants. When an MP places a PQ, this triggers an information-gathering system in a department of state, with a Principal based in the Secretary of State's private office or in the parliamentary section of the department co-ordinating the process, consulting with colleagues throughout the department (on occasions right down to local branch level), drafting the text of the answer and, in the case of oral PQs, listing possible supplementaries.

It would be quite wrong to view this as a purely mechanical process, with no meaning as far as the accountability of civil servants is concerned. While, ultimately, the PQ system is about calling ministers to account to Parliament, it also focuses attention on the work of officials at various levels of a departmental hierarchy. PQs about a policy initiative, the management of part of a department or the implementation of policy might be likened to searchlights (some of which are, admittedly, brighter than others!) which cast beams into the dark reaches of officialdom, thereby obliging civil servants to enlighten their ministers and official superiors about the actions they have or have not been taking. The internal accountability of civil servants is thus enhanced by the PQ system, sporadic though it may be, and it can be argued that a form of indirect external accountability of officials to Parliament is also made possible by the PQ.

A similar effect is created by the demands of standing committees, which examine Bills clause by clause (Norton, 1981; 1993; Drewry, 1988a), and by the various types of parliamentary debate (Norton, 1993), which serve the purpose of bringing ministers to account in broad and specific terms for their proposed legislation (in the case of Second and Third Reading debates) or for elements of government policy and administrative action (via debates on the Queen's Speech, government motions, opposition motions, estimates days and adjournment motions).

These devices illustrate the important role played by civil servants as policy advisers, departmental managers and policy administrators in the sense that a small number of senior officials will accompany the minister when he or she attends the standing committee or the debate. Of course, these officials are not full participants: as far as the official verbatim records of proceedings and broadcast reports are concerned, the civil servants do not exist.

However, the mute observers who sit behind their ministers in the standing committee rooms and at the side of the chamber during Commons debates are there to help their political chiefs as they account to Parliament. The officials play their part by preparing verbal and documentary briefings for ministers in advance of the parliamentary appearances, and by passing notes of guidance to ministers in the course of the committee sessions and debates. However, civil servants are directly, legally and constitutionally accountable to Parliament for one key element of departmental management: finance. A senior official in every department of state, usually the Permanent Secretary, is designated the Accounting Officer, with responsibility for ensuring that proper accounting conventions have been observed, and public funds granted by Parliament have been safeguarded and spent with due attention being paid to economy, efficiency and effectiveness. The Accounting Officer must keep ministers fully informed about the financial implications of policy initiatives, in the knowledge that the Comptroller and Auditor General and his or her staff in the National Audit Office (who act as agents of Parliament) will scrutinise the departmental accounts, and place reports before the Public Accounts Committee (PAC) of the House of Commons (Flegman, 1980; 1985; Latham, 1986; Robinson, 1988).

The PAC, which is the oldest (it dates from 1861) and most prestigious of the Commons select committees, examines departmental Accounting Officers in considerable detail on matters arising from the accounts, paying particular attention to problematic items which have been identified by the National Audit Office. The hearings conducted by the PAC therefore provide us with the only evidence of undisputed *de jure* direct accountability of civil servants to Parliament. There are no opportunities for officials to 'pass the buck' to ministers in this forum. Indeed, the Accounting Officer's Memorandum, which is issued to Permanent Secretaries, stresses the personal nature of the civil servant's accountability for these matters, and sets out in some detail the steps to be followed by an Accounting Officer who has reservations about a minister's spending plans. Should the latter involve financial irregularity or impropriety in the opinion of the Accounting Officer, and should the minister decide to overrule the written objections of the official, the expenditure will be allowed, but an Accounting Officer's Minute should be sent to the Treasury and the Comptroller and

Auditor General. This action will have the effect of exempting the Accounting Officer from the accountability enforced by the PAC, in relation to that specific item of expenditure.

It is extremely rare for this procedure to be invoked. The clearest and best-documented case involved a major disagreement between Tony Benn, the Secretary of State for Industry, and his Permanent Secretary, Sir Antony Part, in 1974–5. Part opposed a number of Benn's plans to use the department's funds in order to support workers' co-operatives, and distanced himself from the minister's policy by issuing Accounting Officer's Minutes (Benn, 1990).

There is certain irony in the fact that Tony Benn's Permanent Secretary was prepared to invoke this procedure in order to avoid being held accountable for elements of ministerial spending which were linked to policy initiatives, while sixteen years later senior Treasury officials failed to distance themselves from a rather personal ministerial spending initiative. In 1991 the Chancellor of the Exchequer, Norman Lamont, was paid £4,700 from Treasury funds to meet part of his legal bill in connection with the eviction of a 'sex therapist' from his London home. The Permanent Secretary of the Treasury, Sir Peter Middleton, and his immediate successor, Sir Terry Burns, were later criticised by the PAC, which recommended a review of the principles and procedures for meeting ministerial expenses:

> There must always be the clearest possible distinction between the use of public funds or resources used to meet expenses incurred . . . in the direct conduct of their official duties, or arising directly from their official position, and the use of such funds for other expenses. . . . On all important matters decisions should be taken by senior officials, normally the accounting officer. (Committee of Public Accounts, 1993: para. 25)

Civil servants have found themselves increasingly being called to account to MPs through the operation of the departmental select committees, established in their modern form in 1979.

Although the House of Commons had traditionally utilised the select committee device for the purpose of specific investigations, and, as we have seen, the Public Accounts Committee had become a firmly entrenched feature of the parliamentary landscape even before the end of the nineteenth century, it was not until the

Table 6.1   House of Commons departmental select committees

Agriculture
Defence
Education[1]
Employment
Environment
Foreign Affairs
Health[2]
Home Affairs
National Heritage[3]
Science and Technology[3]
Scottish Affairs[4]
Social Security[2]
Trade and Industry
Transport
Treasury and Civil Service
Welsh Affairs

Notes [1] Education, Science and Arts, 1979–92
        [2] Social Services, 1979–90
        [3] New select committees, appointed in July 1992. Energy Committee abolished.
        [4] Not reappointed, 1987–92, due to dispute about its composition.

mid-1960s that an attempt was made to set up a series of select committees with fairly wide-ranging remits to scrutinise areas of the government machine. The 'experimental' select committees of 1966–70 (some of which survived into the 1970s) and the broadly based Expenditure Committee of the 1970s represented a rather fitful development of this form of scrutiny.

The major reform of 1979, spearheaded by the Leader of the House of Commons, Norman St John Stevas, saw the advent of fourteen departmentally based select committees, each of which had a guaranteed lifespan of at least one parliamentary session, and had powers to call for witnesses, papers and records, and publish reports (Drewry, 1988b). By 1992, the configuration of select committees had altered to some extent (see Table 6.1), but the select committee system had clearly emerged as a vitally important means of parliamentary accountability.

The significance of the select committees for the civil service was not inconsiderable: more officials than ever before were being called in person to answer questions from MPs, with positive consequences for internal lines of accountability back in the departments of state, as memoranda of evidence were compiled and briefing papers were written for the witnesses. Beyond this, it could be argued that the cumulative impact of the post-1979 regime of select committees was a challenge to the *de jure* non-accountability of officials to Parliament, to the point where a developing *de facto* accountability could be discerned. After all, unlike Parliamentary Questions, debates or meetings of standing committees, select committee hearings provided opportunities for civil servants to be directly questioned in person.

Extreme caution is required when considering the concept of civil service accountability to Parliament, however, and we must attach a note of qualification to the comments above. Civil servants giving evidence to select committees are expected to adhere to the guidelines set out in a Memorandum of Guidance for Officials Appearing Before Select Committees, usually referred to as the Osmotherly Memorandum. First compiled by Edward Osmotherly, an official in the old Civil Service Department, in 1980, and periodically updated under the auspices of the Cabinet Office since then, the Osmotherly Memorandum specifically precludes officials from offering comments on the operation of Cabinet Committees, the legal departments, inter-departmental policy communications, policy advice given to ministers or matters of political controversy. This document has been described as 'twenty five pages of how to say "I'm sorry, Chairman. I can't answer that question. May I refer you to my Minister?"' (Hennessy and Smith, 1992: 16). In practice, Osmotherly is only occasionally invoked as a stalling device by civil servants who wish to escape close questioning by select committees. More important, perhaps, is the ethos conjured up by such a document, which seems to represent the spirit of a former civil service, one in which the concepts of 'facelessness' and 'anonymity' held much more significance than today. There was some expectation that the anachronistic character of the Osmotherly Memorandum would be attacked by the Select Committee on Procedure in the course of its major review of the working of the select committee system in 1990 (Select Committee on Procedure, 1990). However, the Procedure Committee seemed to take the view that it would be better to let sleeping dogs lie, since Osmotherly had not limited the ability of select committees to scrutinise effectively, and any revised Memorandum might be enforced more rigorously, to the disadvantage of the select committees (Judge, 1992).

The founder of the post-1979 system, Norman St John Stevas, clearly regretted this missed opportunity to lay Osmotherly to rest:

> It was extremely feeble of them to bow down and worship the Osmotherly rules as though they were the law. What they should have said was, these rules are out of date, they came into existence in an entirely different situation, they could be swept away entirely and we should start again. . . . That would have been a splendid thing to do. (Hennessy and Smith, 1992: 16)

The existence of a slightly less formal encouragement to civil servants to place limits on their co-operation with select committees was revealed in 1993. BBC Television's *Scrutiny* programme, which reports on the activities of parliamentary committees, uncovered a civil service training video, made in 1987 under the auspices of the Director of Training at the Central Office of Information, which briefs officials on techniques to adopt when giving evidence to select committees (BBC *Scrutiny*, 1993). The words of Sir Brian Hayes, Permanent Secretary at the Department of Trade and Industry, confirmed certain MPs' views about the stalling tactics of at least some civil service witnesses:

> I don't think it is a good idea just to answer yes because then they go straight on to another question and you're foxed again. It also, of course, fills in a certain amount of time and one remembers all these committees have, as it were, a finishing time. (BBC *Scrutiny*, 1993)

Most members of select committees appeared to have been ignorant of the existence of this video, and a minor storm brewed up when it became clear that communications between select committee clerks and departmental liaison officers charged with the conduct of relations with the select committees extended in some cases to the provision of advance notification of some lines of questioning (*The Guardian*, 1993).

None the less, despite the qualifications and reservations which must be expressed, we would be justified in reaching the conclusion that the experience of scrutiny by select committee has produced a quantitative and qualitative enhancement of civil service accountability.

Another organ of parliamentary scrutiny which was introduced in the 1960s, at the same time as the first wave of experimental select committees, and which was to have a significant impact on civil service accountability was the Parliamentary Commissioner for Administration (Gregory and Hutchesson, 1975; Gregory and Pearson, 1992).

The Parliamentary Commissioner for Administration Act, 1967, created this UK 'Ombudsman'. The PCA receives complaints, through MPs, from members of the public about alleged maladministration by government departments and associated bodies. The concept of maladministration is rather vague, and, in practice, the Commissioner can exercise an element of discretion when interpreting the term. Having satisfied himself that the subject of the complaint falls within his jurisdiction, relates to a department or body covered by his remit, and there is no alternative avenue of redress open to the complainant, the Commissioner will launch an investigation which can involve the direct questioning of ministers and civil servants (although not in public) and the examination of all relevant documents and records relating to the case in question (with the exception of papers from the Cabinet or any of its committees). His investigation complete, the PCA files a report with the MP who referred the complaint and the Permanent Secretary of the department concerned, and incorporates an anonymised summary version of the case in his quarterly report to Parliament. The report will have cleared the department of the charge of maladministration, or delivered a 'guilty' verdict, in which case remedial action (up to and including financial compensation) will be recommended. A third possible conclusion is for the PCA to clear the department of maladministration *per se*, while finding some fault with its administrative procedures. Figure 6.1 sets out the way in which complaints were processed by the PCA in 1993.

The 'parliamentary' nature of the PCA can be seen in several respects. First, the Commissioner and his staff are technically servants of Parliament (although the Commissioner is formally appointed by the government and the Chairman of the Select Committee on the PCA is only consulted). Richard Crossman, the Leader of the House of Commons, commended the PCA to MPs on the grounds that this would 'put at the disposal of the backbench Member an extremely sharp and piercing instrument of investigation' (Crossman, 1966: col. 60). This public statement notwithstanding, it was typical of Crossman that he would confide to his diary on the same day his reservations about the limited powers of the PCA (Crossman, 1976: 76)!

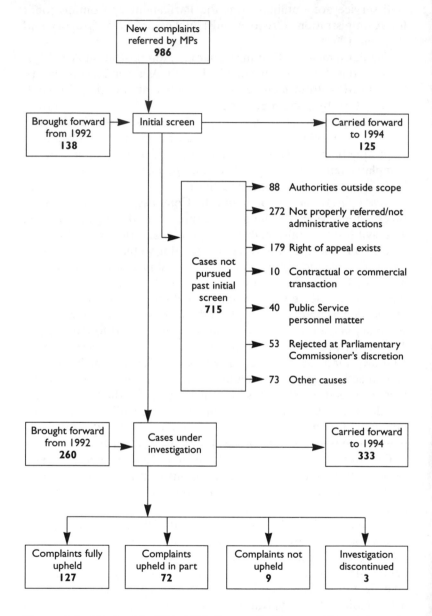

Figure 6.1 Work of the PCA, 1993. (Source: Parliamentary Commissioner for Administration, Annual Report 1994)

Secondly, there is no direct access to the PCA, unlike Ombudsmen in other countries: access is via the MP 'filter' (this system has been the subject of a long-running debate, with supporters of the filter arguing that this guarantees a higher quality of service, and opponents asserting that it inhibits many potential complainants).

Finally, the PCA reports to Parliament and, lacking legal power of enforcement for his decisions, relies on the Commons Select Committee on the PCA to follow-up his recommendations and put pressure on recalcitrant departments.

Despite certain limitations, it can be argued that the PCA has had a definite impact on the accountability of civil servants to Parliament. After 1967 it became possible for officials at every level of the departmental hierarchy to be directly questioned about the discharge of their responsibilities in relation to particular cases. Table 6.2 provides a breakdown of the numbers of complaints passed onto the PCA by MPs, cases investigated and complaints upheld, over the first twenty-seven years of the scheme. The practical operation of the PCA system would bear out Crossman's bold assertion during the Second Reading debate on the Bill:

> for the first time a complaint to a back-bench Member of Parliament about maladministration in any Department may precipitate a searching and detailed investigation, including the close examination of everyone concerned, from the top to the bottom of the Department and the examination of all the relevant secret Departmental files. (Crossman, 1966: col. 59)

As Gregory has pointed out, the private questioning of civil servants by the Commissioner or members of his staff can be supplemented, if the department refuses to grant a remedy recommended by the PCA in order to redress citizens' grievances, by the public questioning of the Permanent Secretary in a meeting of the Select Committee on the PCA (Gregory, 1982: 56).

Permanent Secretaries respond to complaints against their departments by guiding the PCA and his staff to the relevant people and files (this task is carried out by a 'nominated officer' who has responsibility for PCA liaison) while simultaneously launching their own investigations, which serve as an official check on the accuracy of the PCA's findings, and, of course, strengthen internal lines of accountability. For the departments which are the major targets of PCA investigations (see Table 6.3) a virtually continuous process of administrative audit is the result.

Table 6.2 Parliamentary Commissioner for Administration, cases 1967–93

	Received via MPs	Investigated	Complaints upheld	% Upheld
1967	1,069	188	19	10.1
1968	1,120	374	38	10.2
1969	761	302	48	15.9
1970	645	259	59	22.8
1971	548	182	67	36.8
1972	573	261	79	30.3
1973	571	239	88	36.8
1974	704	252	94	37.3
1975	928	244	90	36.9
1976	815	320	139	43.4
1977	901	312	111	35.6
1978	1,259	341	131	38.4
1979	758	223	84	37.7
1980	1,031	225	107	47.6
1981	917	228	104	45.6
1982	838	202	67	33.2
1983	751	198	83	41.9
1984	837	183	81	44.3
1985	759	177	75	42.4
1986	719	168	82	48.8
1987	677	145	63	43.5
1988	701	120	59	49.2
1989	677	126	61	48.4
1990	704	177	74	41.8
1991	801	183	87	47.5
1992	945	196	103	52.6
1993	986	211	127	60.2

Sources: Gregory and Pearson (1992); PCA (1993, 1994).

While the great majority of cases handled by the PCA concern relatively low-key matters of alleged administrative or managerial failing, there have been a number of high-profile cases in the period since 1967, the investigation of which has served to focus public attention on the actions of ministers and civil servants alike. The main examples would be the following:

- *Sachsenhausen:* a case where the Foreign Office had repeatedly denied payment to a group of former prisoners of war who claimed that they came within the terms of the

Table 6.3 Main departments investigated by the PCA, 1993

Department	% of total referrals	Complaints	Investigations
Social Security	30	299	85
Inland Revenue	16	156	64
Environment	6	59	5
Transport	6	59	15
Customs and Excise	5	48	10
Lord Chancellor's	3	30	9
Home Office	3	27	7
Trade and Industry	3	26	5

Source: Parliamentary Commissioner for Administration (1994).

government's compensation scheme for inmates of Nazi concentration camps (Parliamentary Commissioner for Administration, 1968).

- *Invalid carriages:* a case where the Department of Health had been slow to commission and publish the results of safety tests on vehicles manufactured and sold under its auspices (Parliamentary Commissioner for Administration, 1974).
- *Television licences:* a bungled attempt by the Home Office to increase licence fees while denying members of the public the chance to purchase licences at the low rate in advance of the official date of the increase (Parliamentary Commissioner for Administration, 1975a).
- *Court line:* a case which involved complaints from people who believed that Department of Trade statements had misled them about the viability of a holiday firm, which suddenly collapsed (Parliamentary Commissioner for Administration, 1975b).
- *Barlow Clowes:* wherein the collapse of a financial investment company which had been issued with a licence by the Department of Trade and Industry brought financial ruin to thousands of investors (Parliamentary Commissioner for Administration, 1989).

It should be noted that although the government explicitly rejected the conclusions reached by the PCA in the Sachsenhausen and Barlow Clowes cases, redress of grievances was at least partially secured through the payment of compensation in each case, in line with the Commissioner's recommendations.

Although officials are not publicly 'named and blamed' in the published reports of the Commissioner, the branches or sections of the departments concerned are invariably the subject of adverse press comment, and, within the small Whitehall 'village' community, the civil servants involved are easily identifiable.

Courts, tribunals and inquiries

Having shown that the external accountability of civil servants to Parliament is a rather patchy, albeit steadily evolving concept, we can now turn our attention to extra-parliamentary aspects of accountability and redress of grievances. Our purpose here is not to examine the detailed operation of the legal and quasi-legal avenues of accountability and redress, which apply to public bodies as a whole and not solely to central government, but simply to offer some general comments on the broad implications of these for the civil service.

In brief, it can be argued that each of the civil servant's possible role responsibilities, for policy advice, departmental and agency management, and policy implementation, may be touched by the systems of legal and quasi-legal accountability.

Dawn Oliver offers a useful summary of the part played by the courts in checking the actions of government:

> Judicial proceedings impose 'explanatory accountability' by requiring public bodies to justify their actions in legal terms; since judicial remedies are enforceable, they also impose amendatory accountability. The courts exercise this power to impose legal accountability through what has come to be known as 'judicial review'. (Oliver, 1991: 111)

The process by which policy decisions are reached, and the procedures for implementation, may be examined by the courts. An example of the effect of judicial review can be seen in the case of *Laker Airways* v. *the Department of Trade* in 1977, when the Court of Appeal held that the policy guidance given by the Secretary of State (on the advice of his officials) to the Civil Aviation Authority to the effect that British Airways should be the only UK airline to serve the route to the United States was in conflict with the 1971 Civil Aviation Act.

The enormous growth in applications to seek judicial review (from under 200 per year in the mid-1970s, to nearly 1,600 per year in the late 1980s) led to civil servants being provided with official guidance (in the form of the 1987 Cabinet Office/Treasury Solicitor's Department publication, *The Judge Over Your Shoulder*) on how to deal with this type of challenge (Garrett, 1992).

There exists no formal code of judicial review; instead, the grounds and rules for review have been developed in a piecemeal, case-by-case fashion over the past century, and have come to include the categories of illegality, procedural impropriety, irrationality or unreasonableness and the abuse of power. This *ad hoc* approach leads some critics to argue for the introduction of, *inter alia*, a codification of the grounds for judicial review, special training for judges hearing these cases, and, more broadly, the advent of a formal system of administrative law allied perhaps to a new Bill of Rights.

Inquiries and tribunals tend to deal with the bread-and-butter elements of administrative life. The former come in many shapes, but are typified by the Planning Inquiries which cover, for example, the compulsory purchase of land or property. Inspectors take evidence and publish reports, which may or may not be heeded by ministers. Tribunals deal with the aftermath of administrative action. A Council on Tribunals oversees a complex system of bodies, some of which exist to resolve dispute between members of the public and official bodies, and propose solutions in disputes involving, for example, Benefit Agency officials or Inspectors of Taxes.

Again, as far as civil servants are concerned, the importance of these bodies lies in the fact that they bring about an element of public accountability and provide for the possibility of redress of grievances caused through official action or inaction.

The Citizen's Charter

The most recent development in the sphere of public accountability and redress of grievances, the Citizen's Charter, was launched in 1991. As we saw, in Chapter 5, the Charter's fundamental objectives were to bring about an improved quality of service delivery and to facilitate more effective redress of grievances.

Some of the concepts and themes associated with the Citizen's Charter were clearly linked to the broader managerial changes taking place in the civil service. However, in the context of the prevailing concern of this chapter, accountability and redress, we can note once again the apparent tension between the constitutionally limited accountability of officials (to ministers and their administrative superiors) and the advent of a by no means clearly defined line of accountability to the 'citizens', or more accurately perhaps, the customers or recipients of services. The constitutional bottom line remains unchanged, but the Citizen's Charter does appear to represent something more than a flirtation with the concept of direct civil service accountability to the public, at least for the service delivery, policy execution or policy implementation role.

Enhanced public accountability and redress of grievances was to be achieved through several linked initiatives within the Charter (Citizen's Charter, 1992: 49–54). The first step was to ensure that existing complaints schemes were brought into line with the Charter's principles of effectiveness, accessibility, simplicity, speediness, objectivity and confidentiality. A Complaints Task Force composed of 'outsiders' was established in 1993, with the purpose of providing advice on setting up and improving complaints systems.

Beyond this, the Citizen's Charter Unit commissioned research which showed that people wishing to find out or complain about public services require basic information about where to go and who to contact in order to resolve their enquiry or problem. Consequently, a pilot telephone helpline scheme, 'Charterline', was introduced in Nottinghamshire, Derbyshire and Leicestershire in 1993, with a view to a national launch in 1994. 'Charterline' offered general information about all published Charters and statements of service standards, as well as contact numbers to help people find out more about public services or make complaints. Where appropriate, callers were to be directed to other sources of help, including the Parliamentary Commissioner for Administration and the Health Service Commissioner. However, much to the government's embarrassment, 'Charterline' was scrapped before reaching the stage of a national launch. In the course of the pilot scheme, it dealt with only 25 calls per day, at a cost to the taxpayer of £68 for each enquiry. To make matters worse, some of the callers seemed to have misunderstood the purpose of the exercise. One man rang to find out how he could take a sperm test. Another, who had apparently been pestered by his mother to the point of distraction, wanted to know how he could become a monk! The under-worked telephone operator obliged by providing the number of a local monastery (Bates and Goodwin, 1994).

In the early stages of its development, what seems to the observer most significant about the Citizen's Charter is probably the spirit which it epitomises rather than any hard-and-fast improvements in accountability. In order to reach anything approaching a definitive judgement on the latter, it would be necessary to monitor the Charter in full operation over a reasonably extended period. For the time being, we can reflect upon the numerous political and academic criticisms which this initiative has attracted (it has been viewed as a mere 'window-dressing' exercise which utilises a very limited and inappropriate concept of citizenship, a scheme which is fatally flawed due to the fact that the service standards are set by the providers of services themselves and are not legally enforceable, and a political gimmick which offers minor consolation prizes in lieu of genuine redress of grievances), and set these against the bold claims made for the Charter by the Prime Minister. We can note that the Citizen's Charter does not establish substantially new organs of accountability or systems for redressing grievances, but instead seeks to facilitate a smoother working of extant organs and shed fresh light on existing avenues of redress.

The fundamental spirit of the Charter nevertheless represents an assertion of the answerability of civil servants (and their political masters) to the public, a commitment to constant internal scrutiny of standards of service provision within government departments and agencies and a willingness (or at least a preparedness) on the part of the official machine to be exposed to a wider and more public scrutiny of its activities. To this extent, it seems fair to conclude that the Citizen's Charter, even in the early phase of its development, stands as a positive step in the direction of enhanced external accountability of the civil service.

The impact of Next Steps

In February 1988, when announcing her government's commitment to the introduction of the Next Steps initiative, Prime Minister Margaret Thatcher made it clear that she saw no need for any amendment of the constitutional rules on accountability. Individual ministerial responsibility would remain sacrosanct, and there would be 'no change in the arrangements for accountability' (Thatcher, 1988). This view was reiterated a few months later when the government responded to a constitutional query by the Treasury and Civil Service Select Committee by making it clear that it

> does not envisage that setting up Executive Agencies within depart-ments will result in changes to the existing constitutional arrange-ments. The further delegation of authority to managers inherent in the Next Steps concept concerns internal accountability within de-partments and does not conflict with the external accountability of Ministers to Parliament. (Treasury and Civil Service Committee, 1988b: 9)

Hostile commentators (Davies and Willman, 1991; McDonald, 1992) viewed this continuing commitment to ministerial respon-sibility, and the failure to take the opportunity afforded by Next Steps to introduce formal direct accountability of civil servants to Parliament, as a fatal flaw at the heart of the programme. Davies and Willman saw the existing constitutional rules on accountability as 'incompatible with the managerialist philosophy of Next Steps' (Davies and Willman, 1991: 27). According to this interpretation, the increased delegation of responsibility for policy execution/ implementation and organisational management to officials work-ing in the new agencies would have to be accompanied by new arrangements for parliamentary scrutiny of civil servants if an ac-countability deficit was to be avoided.

What is the truth about Next Steps? Has it opened up an 'ac-countability gap' through which ministers and civil servants can slip, thus avoiding detailed parliamentary scrutiny of their ac-tivities? Conversely, does it perhaps facilitate clearer identification of responsibilities, thus enhancing accountability?

Let us turn our attention, in the first instance, to the implications of Next Steps for internal accountability. In general terms, each agency Chief Executive is accountable to the Secretary of State in the parent department for the specific responsibilities delegated to the agency under the terms of the Framework Document. At least in the sphere of financial management, there is also an element of accountability to the Permanent Secretary of the parent depart-ment, in his capacity as Accounting Officer, although, as we shall see, this is complicated by the fact that some agencies have greater financial independence than others. The delegated responsibilities normally cover the delivery of a particular service, execution or implementation of policy in a given sphere (a simple example being the Benefits Agency's responsibilities in the field of social security), together with the management of budgets, personnel and other resources at the disposal of the agency. Meanwhile, back in the parent departments, the new freedom from day-to-day concerns with policy execution and service delivery, would create scope for a second wave of managerial rationalisation.

Ideally, therefore, Next Steps was to bring about a clearer identification of role responsibilities in both parent departments and agencies, thus enhancing internal systems of accountability, while simultaneously conferring greater autonomy on agency Chief Executives and their management boards.

While it would be wrong to deny that some clarification of internal lines of accountability did occur as a result of Next Steps, particularly in the realm of service delivery and policy implementation, the initiative did not invariably lead to clarity. In the management sphere, lines of accountability seemed to become somewhat tangled.

The managerial autonomy granted to Chief Executives in relation to matters of recruitment, pay and conditions of service did not differ fundamentally from the 'flexibilities' allowed under the new, civil-service-wide, managerial regime (with the exception of a small number of cases, where arrangements specific to a particular agency would be set out in the Framework Document). Indeed, there were some indications that the agencies were being tied fairly tightly into the managerial structures and processes of the parent departments, thus defeating at least one of the objects of the exercise: to untangle and clarify managerial responsibilities.

Successive surveys conducted by Price Waterhouse indicated an element of concern within the agencies about the amount of time being given over to matters relating to targets, budgets and personnel management (Price Waterhouse, 1991; 1992). The close department–agency links have also been commented upon by Davies and Willman:

> Agencies complained that the amount of control exercised by the centre has increased rather than decreased since they were set up. Departments exert a further brake on Agencies' independence by requirements in the [so-called] Framework Document that the

Agency must procure certain services from the central department. . . . Where Agencies are based out of London, as with Companies House or the Vehicle Inspectorate it would be financially
advantageous and often more convenient to obtain these services
locally. (Davies and Willman, 1991: 31)

The Fraser Report, which reviewed the first three years of the Next
Steps initiative, commented unfavourably upon the compulsory provision of services by departments without adequate costing, and
recommended the introduction of proper charging and invoicing
arrangements, and, where possible value-for-money comparisons
with services on offer from outside the department (Efficiency Unit,
1991). Incidentally, the Fraser Report also sounded some alarm
bells about the paucity of managerial change accomplished in the
parent departments since the launching of the initiative.

The introduction of market testing provided yet another illustration of the close managerial links between parent departments and
agencies. It has been possible to detect a grumbling resentment on
the part of Chief Executives, who believe that the manner in which
market testing was introduced was an infringement upon the concept of devolved management. Agencies and Chief Executives
might have been left to decide upon their own priorities instead of
having a quota (25 per cent of all activities) for market testing
imposed upon them.

If internal lines of accountability were, at best, only partially
untangled and strengthened as a consequence of Next Steps, what
of external accountability to Parliament? Although it was meant to
clarify the respective responsibilities of ministers and civil servants, there was a sense in which the Next Steps initiative came up
against a long-standing problem: the difficulty in differentiating
between matters of policy on the one hand (for which ministers
and senior civil servants might be held accountable), and operational matters on the other (for which agency Chief Executives
and their staffs might be held accountable). Patricia Greer cites the
example of a very basic, ostensibly operational matter in which
ministers came to take a close interest due to its political sensitivity: the layout of local Benefits Agency offices, whether there
should be glass screens and the amount of privacy required for
customers (Greer, 1994: 88). The general point is that the dividing
line between policy and matters relating to its implementation, is
blurred.

Does 'policy' stop at the high level of agenda setting or are the tools with which policies are implemented, the policy instruments, also to be defined as 'policy'? Equally, who is to be held accountable for ministers acting on poor quality policy advice – the ministers for taking that advice or the civil servants for providing it? (Greer, 1994: 87)

The government's expressed will that extant notions of constitutional accountability should not be tampered with still allowed agency Chief Executives and their staffs to be questioned by select committees (with the Osmotherly rules in operation, of course) and to be subject to investigation by the Parliamentary Commissioner for Administration in the same manner as civil servants in conventional departments of state.

However, complications set in with regard to two other avenues of parliamentary scrutiny, the Public Accounts Committee and Parliamentary Questions. The government initially took the view that there was no need to amend the arrangement whereby the Permanent Secretary of a department, in his capacity as Accounting Officer, answered to the PAC for all aspects of departmental finances, including those relating to agencies associated with the department. This did not seem to be in line with the spirit of Next Steps, which allocated financial management responsibilities to Chief Executives. Following a request from the Treasury and Civil Service Select Committee, the government agreed that agency Chief Executives should be given the status of Accounting Officers, in two categories. Chief Executives of those agencies which had substantial financial independence from the parent department (due to the fact that they were categorised as Trading Funds and were responsible for raising much of their own finance through charging for services or products, or were funded through a separate parliamentary Vote) would be appointed by the Treasury to be Accounting Officers in their own right. Chief Executives of agencies which remained linked into the parent department's financial system (because they are funded through one or more of the department's parliamentary Votes) would be designated Agency Accounting Officers by the Permanent Secretary of the parent department.

The effect of this was to ensure that Agency Accounting Officers would be accompanied by the departmental Permanent Secretary when giving evidence to the PAC. Both the Fraser Report and the

Seventh Report from the Treasury and Civil Service Select Committee in 1990–1 argued that this formulation created uncertainty about the respective financial responsibilities of Chief Executives and Permanent Secretaries (Efficiency Unit 1991: 8; Treasury and Civil Service Committee 1991a: paras 86–8), but the Agency Accounting Officer designation remained.

The explicit division of the policy-making and policy-execution functions which, at least in theory, lay at the heart of the Next Steps initiative, seemed to promise the clearer identification of officials responsible for specific aspects of service delivery (bearing in mind the problems associated with this distinction between policy and service delivery, cited above). Members of Parliament were informed that they could expect to receive replies to their letters and Parliamentary Questions on matters related to the day-to-day work of agencies, from the relevant Chief Executives, rather than from the departmental ministers. Thus, any given letter or PQ on an agency submitted to a minister for written answer would be examined by the minister's Private Office in order to determine whether the topic of the enquiry fell within the range of matters which were the remit of the parent department (strategic policy or finance, for example) or of the agency (the service delivered to one of the MP's constituents by the local branch office of the agency, for example). If the latter, the MP's letter or PQ would be passed on to the Chief Executive. A PQ pertaining to an agency's sphere of responsibility, but submitted for oral answer, would merely elicit a verbal response from the minister on the floor of the House, to the effect that the matter was being passed on to the Chief Executive.

Now, while most MPs did not seem to object to receiving replies to their letters from Chief Executives, and, indeed, MPs generally followed the government's guidelines by submitting such letters directly to the Chief Executives in the first instance, the new arrangement for answering PQs caused something of a constitutional tussle.

Discontent stemmed from the fact that, before Next Steps, PQs for written answer which related to policy execution or service delivery would have been answered, at least formally, by the appropriate minister, and placed on the public record through publication in *Hansard*. Oral PQs would, of course, have brought the minister to the floor of the House, where he could be exposed to further scrutiny via supplementaries. Now, Chief Executives would account for such matters in letters of reply to the MPs raising the issues. In 1990, the government agreed that copies of these replies would, as a matter of course, be placed in the Library of the House of Commons, for ease of access by all MPs (previously, a reply had been placed in the Library only when this was specifically requested by the MP concerned). Some MPs were dismayed by what they saw as a dilution of ministerial accountability and answerability, and were not convinced that the new arrangements would lead to greater efficiency. The Labour MP Gerald Kaufman mounted something of a campaign against a system which he believed was producing further delays in securing answers, and removing a fundamental right of MPs:

> I want all of us, when we raise an individual case concerning our constituents, to have that case considered by a minister. Members of Parliament have no power and only two rights. One is the right of privileged speech within Parliament. The other is the right of access to ministers. We exercise those rights not for ourselves but on behalf of our constituents. If ministers seek to eliminate one of those rights, as they are doing by delegating cases to agencies, units and officials, they are diminishing the rights of our constituents and the rights of Parliament. They are diminishing democracy. (Kaufman, 1992)

Kaufman was attacking the idea that Chief Executives should answer either MPs' letters or PQs; he wanted to deal with ministers, not officials, in every case. However, even those who supported the logic of requiring Chief Executives to answer for the activities of their agencies, and were not necessarily unhappy to receive letters from Chief Executives in response to their own missives, pointed to the deficiencies of a system which produced formal letters for consultation by MPs only, instead of published responses to PQs in *Hansard* which could be read by any member of the public. The Treasury and Civil Service Select Committee led the attack on this obvious weakness of the new arrangements.

> Replies from the Chief Executive, even if placed in the Library of the House, are not freely available to those outside the House. . . . If the current procedure for answering Members' questions continues to cause problems we would expect that the Government would consider introducing an appropriate mechanism whereby the replies of Chief Executives arising from questions tabled to Ministers could be published. . . . There is a danger that, despite the

wholly laudable intention of making those responsible for carrying out the service fully accountable to Parliament, much information currently available to Parliament and public will no longer be readily accessible. (Treasury and Civil Service Committee, 1990a: paras 68, 70)

The government initially refused to be moved on this issue. The Treasury and Civil Service Select Committee (Treasury and Civil Service Committee, 1991a: paras 74–83) and the Select Committee on Procedure (Select Committee on Procedure, 1991: paras 122–6) pursued the matter, while Paul Flynn MP and the academic Tony Lynes began publishing *Open Lines*, an unofficial edited version of Chief Executives' letters which had been deposited in the Commons Library. Eventually, in November 1991, the government accepted that Chief Executives' replies should be published. After giving some consideration to the mechanics of this, in 1992 the replies of Chief Executives to PQs began to be published in a supplement to *Hansard*.

Leaving aside the technicalities associated with the mechanisms of accountability, as the Next Steps initiative gathered steam, it became clear that some agency Chief Executives were adopting relatively high profiles as they accounted for the work of their agencies. This was particularly noticeable in the case of Ros Hepplewhite, the Chief Executive of the Child Support Agency (CSA). In her numerous dealings with parliamentary inquiries about the operation of this controversial agency, which was charged with the task of securing maintenance payments from absent fathers, Hepplewhite was the antithesis of the 'anonymous', 'unaccountable' civil servant. None the less, she was always at pains to differentiate between her responsibility to account for the management and operation of the agency, and the accountability of ministers for the policy and legal framework within which the agency operated. When it became clear that the CSA had failed to achieve its key targets, and in the wake of revelations that a team of management consultants had been called in to review the management of the agency, Hepplewhite resigned in September 1994.

Having considered the main issues relating to the external accountability of the Next Steps agencies to Parliament, we can see that, to some extent, the government seemed to be trying to have the best of both worlds. On the one hand, the commitment to unchanged notions of constitutional accountability, and, by implication, the non-accountability of civil servants to Parliament (except in special circumstances) was rigorously re-asserted. On the other hand, it appeared that, despite the government's refusal to countenance any formal changes in constitutional accountability, civil servants rather than ministers were to answer directly to MPs for operational matters. For the government, this was a practical matter, which had no constitutional implications and did not detract from ultimate ministerial responsibility. For sceptics and critics there seemed to be an accountability gap in the making, on the lines of the one which had facilitated buck-passing by ministers and the boards of the old nationalised industries. For the detached observer, perhaps the messy, *de facto* accountability of agency Chief Executives to Parliament which seems to be emerging has something in common with the theme examined at an earlier stage in this chapter: the subtle, almost crab-like growth in civil service accountability to Parliament in the real world, even in the face of repeated assertions of constitutional, *de jure*, non-accountability.

It might be argued that systems of accountability and effective redress of grievances can only operate effectively when there is a measure of openness in the governmental process. We now turn our attention to the issue of official secrecy.

7

LETTING THE SUN SHINE IN?
Open government and a culture of secrecy

The civil service operates within a constitutional and political system which, traditionally, has been characterised by an adherence to official secrecy. In the early 1990s there were some indications that this culture might be changing, although many observers remained sceptical about the nature and extent of the change.

The purpose of this chapter is to examine the implications of official secrecy for civil servants, while reviewing the moves towards greater openness and assessing their impact on the civil service.

A tradition of secrecy

The process of government necessarily involves the holding of 'secrets'. Certain types of information, particularly those relating to matters of national security and diplomacy, must be closely guarded if the interests of government and people are to be properly safeguarded. Beyond this, it is often argued that the 'anonymity' of civil servants needs to be preserved if they are to function effectively as impartial advisers to governments of different political complexions, and this cannot be achieved if public exposure is unlimited. A further consideration is the requirement that transactions between government bodies and private-sector organisations remain hidden from view in the interest of preserving commercial interests. Additionally, bureaucracies have a natural tendency to retain information, partly as a means of enhancing the mystique and superiority of the profession.

It can be argued, however, that in Britain there is a tradition of secrecy in government which goes beyond these norms.

> Britain has one of the most extensive systems to control the flow of official information of any Western democracy. . . . A powerful and persistent culture of secrecy – reflecting the basic assumption that good government is closed government and the public should only be allowed to know what the government decides they should know – was carried over from the nineteenth century and refined in the twentieth century when it was given statutory backing through Britain's formidable secrecy laws. (Ponting, 1990: 1)

The legal basis for official secrecy in Britain developed steadily, to the point where over 100 statutes existed to criminalise the unauthorised disclosure of information. The keystones of this system are the Official Secrets Acts of 1911, 1920, 1939 and 1989. However, the statutes are supplemented by an array of conventions, rules and codes which give further emphasis to official secrecy and establish detailed behavioural constraints. Thus, for example, the Thirty Year Rule places a blanket ban on publication of official documents for a period of three decades (and particularly sensitive papers may be withheld for considerably longer periods). The Osmotherly Memorandum sets out a code of behaviour for civil servants appearing as witnesses before House of Commons select committees, and places clear limits on the types of information officials should divulge or even discuss.

A number of historical, political and cultural factors have contributed to the web of secrecy which surrounds the British system of government. Among these, we can cite the following:

- The nature of the British constitution. In particular, the large expanses of the constitution which remain 'unwritten', and are, in consequence, relatively easy to supplement with codes, rules and conventions which reinforce official secrecy. Additionally, the lack of any constitutional 'right to know' hampers members of the public and their representatives when seeking access to official information.

- The convention of collective responsibility, which obliges ministers to support the policies and actions of the government, whatever their personal reservations, and requires them to respect the confidentiality of discussions which take place within departments, the Cabinet or Cabinet committees.

- The tradition and culture of the civil service, which lend themselves to a guarded, extremely wary approach to public scrutiny. In Whitehall, the concept of 'open government' tends to be viewed as a contradiction in terms.

- The adversarial political system, which places a premium on the retention of information which is even remotely likely to embarrass the government.

- The prevalence of international crises and wars throughout most of the twentieth century, which helped create an atmosphere of suspicion and distrust, and cultivated a generally suspicious attitude towards the unnecessary or premature release of information. It is noteworthy that the 1911 Official Secrets Act, the most sweeping secrecy statute of all, was introduced amidst panic about German espionage.

Comparisons between Britain and other liberal democratic states reveal some significant differences in approach (Thomas, 1989). Even the most 'open' system of government will retain a level of secrecy for key areas of activity. Where rights of access to official information exist, the specific procedures to be followed by an individual requesting information, the time limits within which government departments must disclose requested information, and the systems for appealing against denials of requests, all serve to complicate the supposed simplicity of government 'openness'. Notwithstanding these points, there are 'freedom of information' 'sunshine' or 'open government' statutes in some states which give ordinary citizens legal rights of access to all government information not specifically designated as secret. Thus, in Sweden, the United States, Australia and Canada, the onus is on the government to justify withholding information. Civil servants have a clear, positive responsibility to aid people seeking access to official information. Indeed, since 1974, officials in the United States have

been liable to disciplinary sanctions if they wrongly refuse to release information. In Britain, by contrast, the underlying assumption has been that government information is secret unless there is
a specific declaration to the contrary.

The implications of this culture of secrecy are many and wide-
ranging. In general terms, it can be argued that maintaining
unnecessarily high levels of secrecy is not conducive to good
government.

> It makes for manipulative government. . . . It means policy-making
> can be carried on discreetly by those 'in the know' with the min-
> imum of outside consultation. . . . Furthermore, the present exces-
> sive level of secrecy . . . lowers the level of public debate, it distorts
> the role of the media and it seriously hampers the way Parliament
> works. (Ponting, 1989: 50)

At its worst, therefore, official secrecy contributes to faulty policy-
making and inhibits agents of accountability and control.

More specifically, for some civil servants, the culture of secrecy
can have particularly serious implications. It can raise acute ethical
dilemmas and lead to crises of conscience which may be impossible
to resolve satisfactorily.

Ethical dilemmas and crises of conscience

Leaking and whistle-blowing: the constitutional and moral dimensions

It might be argued that civil servants are in a relationship of accountability to four sources: their ministers, their departmental
and agency superiors, Parliament and 'the people'.

However, as we saw in Chapter 6, the constitution only affords
full recognition to the first two of these sources. Direct civil service
accountability to Parliament is strictly limited in formal terms (to
the Accounting Officers who are directly accountable to the Public
Accounts Committee of the House of Commons), although an
emerging, unofficial, *de facto* accountability could be discerned,
particularly in relation to the work of select committees and the
Parliamentary Commissioner for Administration.

What of the possibility of accountability to 'the people' or 'the
public interest'? The constitution makes no allowance for this at

all. Civil servants have no prior duty to the public interest: there exists no constitutional relationship between officialdom and the people.

In constitutional terms, therefore, it is the internal sources of accountability, to their ministers and official superiors, which are of primary significance for civil servants.

Now this begs some further questions. Could there be any circumstances in which a civil servant might come to believe that there should be an opportunity to claim an overriding accountability beyond ministers and official superiors, to the people or their representatives in Parliament? What possible courses of action might be open to an official in this position? Finally, given the constitutional restrictions we have already set out, what sanctions might be imposed on such a civil servant? Let us examine these questions in turn.

While it is undoubtedly true that the constitution brooks no deviation from the concept of civil service accountability to their official superiors and to ministers, it is not too difficult to envisage circumstances in which an official's conscience might lead him or her to invoke an ultimate accountability to the public interest. Indeed, at the beginning of the development of modern theories of civil service accountability, it was argued that some degree of official accountability to the 'public interest', variously defined, was highly desirable in the interest of good government (Friedrich, 1940; Finer, 1941).

Generally speaking, we might conceive of three types of occasion during which a civil servant might wish to invoke an ultimate, overriding accountability, and disclose official information in the public interest. These might arise when an official is confronted with the following:

- Illegal activity.
- Unconstitutional acts.
- A desire to focus attention or fuel debate on politically controversial issues.

Ostensibly, it would seem more defensible for a civil servant to disclose information in order to shed light on corrupt or unconstitutional conduct rather than merely to draw attention to a matter of political controversy. However, we are in the realm of indefinite concepts here, and it should be understood that even those cases which have a basis in legal or constitutional issues can come to take on the characteristics of political controversy. Moreover, it is entirely feasible for a matter which is politically sensitive, but lacks the ingredients of corruption or unconstitutional conduct, to provide a strong *prima facie* case for disclosure.

The most commonly cited instance of disclosure taking place with the specific purpose of fuelling debate on a matter of political controversy involved Desmond Morton, the official head of the government's Industrial Intelligence Centre in the 1930s. Morton leaked information to Winston Churchill, in order to allow him to launch parliamentary attacks on the government's defence policies. Although Churchill would later claim that Morton had been given official permission to keep him informed, by passing on secret information, no evidence ever emerged to support this assertion. On the contrary, as Churchill's biographer has argued, the administrations which were supposedly conniving at this supply of secret and politically sensitive information had nothing to gain, and a great deal to lose, from such a transaction (Gilbert, 1976: 555). The Morton leaks did not seek to expose unconstitutional or illegal acts: they were politically motivated. When the net result of this episode is considered, we can see that there may be cases where the greater good is served by civil servants invoking an ultimate accountability to 'the public interest'. In this sense, in some cases there might be a moral, if not a constitutional, justification for disclosure.

A civil servant who opts for disclosure on moral grounds might choose to do so by openly 'blowing the whistle' or, more surreptitiously, by leaking information or documents. In practice, the existence of a range of punishment sanctions makes leaking, rather than whistle-blowing, the more likely strategy. Whatever the mode of disclosure, the constitutional facts of life are clear: there is no recognised line of accountability from the civil service to 'the people'. Before the eruption of the series of *causes célèbres* we consider in the next section, the punishment sanctions available to governments confronted with unauthorised disclosures fell into three broad categories.

The first contained the internal disciplinary sanctions set out in the Civil Service Pay and Conditions of Service (CSPCS) Code. This contained a section on the 'disclosure of official information', and the discipline section of the old 'Estacode' (which remained extant in the more recent CSPCS Code) set out the sanctions available to the Permanent Secretary of a department. These ranged from a formal reprimand to downgrading or dismissal.

The second category expanded considerably upon the internal sanctions, and introduced the possibility of criminal proceedings. The Official Secrets Acts, and, in particular, the 'catch-all' Section 2 of the 1911 Act, covered any unauthorised disclosure of official information. Such disclosures constituted an offence punishable by up to two years' imprisonment. Unlike the disciplinary proceedings approved by the CSPCS Code, the Official Secrets Acts applied to civil servants in retirement as well as during their careers in the service.

The third category contained the statutory prohibitions on disclosure which applied when a person received payment in return for leaked information.

> The Prevention of Corruption Acts 1906 and 1916 and the Public Bodies Corrupt Practices Act 1899 contain penalties which may be imposed upon individuals who receive or agree to receive a reward in return for a disclosure of information about the activities of their employer. It is possible that an offence may be committed under those Acts even though the disclosure in question is in the public interest and the receipt of a reward is not the reason for the disclosure but merely one of its incidental consequences. (Cripps, 1983: 624)

The cases of Willmore, Tisdall and Ponting

Ethical dilemmas, crises of conscience, constitutional norms and moral imperatives were thrown into sharp relief in the course of sixteen months between the autumn of 1983 and the early part of 1985 (Pyper, 1985). In three separate cases, each with a fundamentally different outcome, the constitutional position of civil servants was placed under detailed scrutiny, and serious questions were raised concerning the efficacy of the existing regime of sanctions in cases of unauthorised disclosure.

The cases unfolded in an atmosphere of high political tension in the period following the re-election of the Thatcher Government in June 1983. In August of that year, each Permanent Secretary received a letter from the then Head of the Civil Service and Secretary to the Cabinet, Sir Robert Armstrong. This blamed the civil service for a spate of leaked documents which had surfaced during the General Election campaign, and asked the Permanent Secretaries to exercise greater vigilance.

Despite intensified efforts to stem the flow of leaks, the months following the distribution of Armstrong's letter saw the publication of a series of newspaper 'exclusives', based on information leaked from a number of different sources within departments of state. Scotland Yard's Serious Crimes Squad was called in, and together with internal government security officers, was instrumental in uncovering three 'moles' over the next few months.

The first 'mole' was to suffer the most severe fate. In October 1983, Sarah Tisdall, a clerk who worked in the office of the Foreign Secretary, anonymously delivered to *The Guardian* two documents written by the Defence Secretary, Michael Heseltine. Each was related to the Greenham Common air base. The newspaper ran stories based on one of the documents: the Foreign Secretary's copy of Heseltine's memorandum to the Prime Minister, which contained information about the expected date of arrival of cruise missiles, as well as details concerning the manner in which the Defence Secretary proposed to handle the announcement in Parliament and before the media.

Tisdall was later to claim that she had leaked the documents because of her general disenchantment with government policies, and her anger at Michael Heseltine's plans for dealing with the public relations aspects of the missiles' arrival. She believed that the memorandum laid bare the Defence Secretary's intention to evade detailed scrutiny in Parliament, by leaving the House of Commons in order to conduct a press conference at the air base, before MPs had a chance to question him in detail about his brief statement.

Following a brief legal struggle (Pyper, 1985: 73), *The Guardian* returned the leaked memorandum to the government in December 1983, possible sources of the leak were speedily identified and, after being interviewed by the police, Sarah Tisdall admitted her offence. In January 1984 she was charged under Section 2 of the 1911 Official Secrets Act. Although offences under this section carry a maximum penalty of three months' imprisonment and a £50 fine if dealt with at a magistrates' court, the government withheld consent for a summary hearing in this type of forum. Instead, Tisdall was tried at the Old Bailey, where, in March 1984, she was found guilty and sentenced to six months in prison.

The case of Ian Willmore was similar to that of Tisdall, in many respects. For each, a general discontentment with government policy was coupled with anger at a specific instance of perceived wrong-doing.

In November 1983, Willmore was an Administration Trainee in the Department of Employment when he read a copy of an informal minute of a meeting between Michael Quinlan (who was about to become Permanent Secretary at the Department of Employment) and Sir John Donaldson, Master of the Rolls. The record of the meeting showed that Donaldson had made suggestions about the possibility of reforming industrial relations law with the aim of introducing further restrictions on the right to strike. Given the constitutional independence of judiciary and executive, such suggestions, if they were to be publicised, would have caused the government considerable embarrassment. Moreover, at the very time Willmore was reading the minute, Donaldson was about to take his place in the Court of Appeal in order to hear, as Master of the Rolls, a particularly sensitive industrial relations case involving a print trade union's appeal against the sequestration of its funds.

Willmore was angered by what he saw as the compromised position of a senior judge, and he sent a copy of the minute to the journal *Time Out*, which published a story based on the affair at the end of November 1983.

An internal investigation was launched, but Willmore attempted to resign before this could reach him. Notwithstanding this, he was interviewed by the Cabinet's chief security adviser, Air Vice Marshall Basil Lock. The evidence against Willmore was insubstantial, and he was prepared to offer a confession only if he was granted immunity from prosecution. The deal was agreed, and Willmore's resignation was accepted early in 1984.

The basic pattern of the Tisdall and Willmore cases was similar. Civil servants saw themselves as having an overriding duty to the public interest which negated their responsibility to the government of the day. Documents were leaked, and sanctions of punishment were imposed (or, in Willmore's case, effectively self-imposed) when the leaks were uncovered.

The pattern was to recur in the case of Clive Ponting. An Assistant Secretary in the Ministry of Defence, Ponting became very disturbed about the manner in which two ministers (the Secretary of State, Michael Heseltine, and the Minister of State, John

Stanley) were dealing with a specific strain of parliamentary inquiries. The circumstances surrounding the sinking of the Argentine cruiser *General Belgrano* during the Falklands War in 1982 remained shrouded with controversy over two years later. The Opposition, individual MPs (especially the indefatigable Labour backbencher Tam Dalyell) and the Foreign Affairs Select Committee continued to pursue the MoD on the details of this matter.

By July 1984 Ponting was quite convinced that his ministers were refusing to answer legitimate questions about the *General Belgrano*, or giving misleading answers and refusing to correct false statements already made to Parliament.

> It dawned on me that I was about the only person who knew all that had happened. Whether I liked it or not I would have to decide what to do. Could I really bring myself to send the documents to Parliament? All my instincts after fifteen years in the Civil Service told me that my loyalty was to Ministers and the department. But then I realised that Ministers had broken their side of the bargain in attempting to evade their responsibilities to Parliament. (Ponting, 1985: 150)

Ponting sent a copy of the key documents to Tam Dalyell, who decided to pass them on to the Foreign Affairs Select Committee, which was in the course of an investigation into the *General Belgrano* affair. To Dalyell's dismay, the Conservative committee chairman handed the papers back to Michael Heseltine, and this triggered an internal MoD investigation, in the course of which Ponting was quickly identified as the 'mole'.

Although he was initially led to believe that he would simply be allowed to resign from the civil service, Ponting was charged under Section 2 of the Official Secrets Act. Basing his defence on the argument that he had acted in the true interests of the state, Ponting was acquitted by the jury at the end of his Old Bailey trial in February 1985 (Ponting, 1985: Chapter 7).

A flawed response: the Armstrong Memorandum

The Tisdall, Willmore and Ponting cases (and, in particular, the adverse publicity which surrounded the Old Bailey trials of Tisdall and Ponting) forced the government to give some consideration to the handling of ethical dilemmas and crises of conscience in the civil service. However, the resultant Note of Guidance on the

Duties and Responsibilities of Civil Servants in Relation to Ministers, written by the Head of the Civil Service, Sir Robert Armstrong, merely emphasised the constitutional norms. The Armstrong Memorandum stressed the dual, internal lines of accountability, stretching from civil servants to their ministerial and official superiors. Civil servants owed to the Crown duties of loyalty and confidentiality. Since the Crown in modern constitutional terms is equated with the government of the day, the position of civil servants could not be distinguished from that of the government. Officials suffering crises of conscience or confronted with ethical dilemmas could not cite an overriding accountability to 'the people' or Parliament. They could consult their senior Establishment Officer (in charge of personnel matters), the Permanent Secretary of the department or even ultimately the Head of the Civil Service, but, if directed to continue working by these individuals, the officials must do so, or resign from the service. Naturally, any civil servant taking the latter course of action would still be liable to prosecution under the Official Secrets Act if he or she made public the reasons for their departure.

This prescription has been openly criticised by retired senior civil servants on a number of occasions. Sir Geoffrey Chipperfield, the former Permanent Secretary of the Department of Energy and the Property Services Agency, commented that:

> the memorandum is full of references to duty but the meaning of the word shifts. . . . High flown sentiments such as these get us nowhere – except to inspire a vague feeling of guilt – but actually stand in the way of good management. (Chipperfield, 1994: 14–15)

At an earlier stage, in 1985, the former Permanent Secretary to the Treasury and joint Head of the Civil Service, Sir Douglas Wass, proposed the establishment of independent appeals procedures to ease the dilemmas of officials suffering from crises of conscience. Wass favoured the device of a civil service 'Ombudsman' or 'Inspector General' (Wass, 1985). Such an innovation would effectively have short-circuited the procedures embodied in the Armstrong Memorandum.

The flawed, inadequate nature of the Armstrong Memorandum was revealed in the course of the Westland affair in 1986 (Pyper, 1987b; Madgwick and Woodhouse, 1989). Colette Bowe, the Director of Information at the Department of Trade and Industry was involved in the leaking of a sensitive document at the height of a politically controversial episode. However, unlike Tisdall, Willmore and Ponting, she leaked at the behest of her minister. The key elements of a letter written by Sir Patrick Mayhew, the Solicitor-General, were released to the press in an attempt to discredit the case for a 'European solution' to the problems of the Westland helicopter company. This case was being championed by Michael Heseltine, the Defence Secretary, in defiance of the wishes of Margaret Thatcher, the Prime Minister, and Leon Brittan, the Secretary of State for Trade and Industry.

It is clear that the conspiracy to discredit Heseltine by means of this leak involved a number of individuals in 10 Downing Street and at the DTI; however, the actual disclosure was to be carried out by Bowe. She had serious qualms about giving unattributable extracts of the Mayhew letter to the Press Association (the Solicitor-General was ignorant of the use to which his private missive was being put). Following the guidance of the Armstrong Memorandum, she attempted to consult her Principal Establishment Officer and her Permanent Secretary, but neither could be contacted, and the pressure mounted on Bowe to get the vital information 'into the public domain'. With a degree of reluctance, she eventually went ahead with the leak. Thus, the practical implementation of the Armstrong Memorandum seemed to be as faulty as its theoretical base!

To some extent, the fact that the Conservatives enjoyed a prolonged period in power after 1979 intensified the ethical issues surrounding ministers and their civil servants. The Armstrong Memorandum did not adequately address the genuine, and growing, concern on the part of many officials that the line between legitimate administrative activities and partisan actions could become blurred. The official guide to ministerial conduct, *Questions of Procedure for Ministers*, clearly states that 'Civil servants should not be asked to engage in activities likely to call in question their political impartiality, or to give rise to the criticism that people paid from public funds are being used for Party political purposes' (Cabinet Office, 1992: para. 55). None the less, as the cases above show, this advice is not invariably followed by ministers. The problem shows no signs of disappearing: from time to time controversy has surrounded research conducted by officials which has been used by ministers in the course of election campaigns to score party political points, and a former head of the Government Statistical Service (Sir Claus Moser) has expressed serious concern about way in which civil servants have been obliged to manipulate data in order to show government policy in the best possible light (Waterhouse, 1989).

A code of ethics?

One possible route away from the problems posed by ethical dilemmas and crises of conscience, much touted by reformers, would be to introduce a new code of ethics, incorporating some form of appeals procedure to allow civil servants to seek independent guidance when confronted with these problems.

The First Division Association and other civil service trade unions have been lobbying for a code of ethics for some time. They have submitted detailed memoranda setting out the content of their proposed code to the Treasury and Civil Service Select Committee (Treasury and Civil Service Committee, 1986; 1993), and given evidence on the importance of this matter to the 'Arms for Iraq' inquiry which was partly concerned with the conduct of civil servants (Scott Inquiry, 1993–4; Norton-Taylor, 1993).

In its interim report, *The Role of the Civil Service*, the Treasury and Civil Service Committee undertook to ascertain the extent to which three key documents provided a satisfactory statement of the constitutional position of the civil service. The three documents to which it referred were the Armstrong Memorandum, the Civil Service Management Code and *Questions of Procedure for Ministers*. In fact, as the Committee noted, the new Civil Service Management Code effectively incorporated the Armstrong Memorandum by stressing the duties of loyalty and life-long confidentiality owed by civil servants to the government. For this reason, it was never likely that the civil service unions would find these documents sufficient basis for a code of ethics. Indeed, in its evidence to the Committee in 1993, the FDA argued that the need for such a code was now a matter of considerable urgency.

For its part, the government adopted a more sanguine approach. William Waldegrave (at that point still Chancellor of the Duchy of Lancaster, with ministerial responsibility for the civil service) was not convinced that the Armstrong Memorandum could be improved upon (Treasury and Civil Service Committee, 1993: para. 18). Meanwhile, Sir Robin Butler gave voice to his belief that the existing guidance offered to civil servants was already sufficiently codified. As for a new appeals procedure – this was patently unnecessary, since only one person had bothered to exercise the existing right of appeal to him, as Head of the Civil Service, in a period of five years (Plowden, 1994: 118). Sir Robin seemed to miss the point that such low usage of the existing mechanism could equally be used to support the contention that it was faulty!

In its White Paper on the civil service, *Continuity and Change*, published in the summer of 1994, the government appeared to leave open the possible future option of a statutory Code (of ethics) 'or even a Civil Service Act' (Prime Minister, 1994: 18). However, this seemed to be an attempt to avoid prejudging any recommendations which might finally emerge from the Treasury and Civil Service Committee, rather than a genuine indication that such new developments were likely.

Some beams of sunlight obscured by clouds?

The 1989 Official Secrets Act – and its limitations

If the cases of Sarah Tisdall and Clive Ponting did much to discredit the Official Secrets Acts (especially the notorious 'catch-all' Section 2 of the 1911 Act), and the general culture of secrecy in British government, the *Spycatcher* affair delivered yet another blow to the system.

This book, which was written by Peter Wright, a former MI5 agent, contained details of the attempts by certain Security Service officers to destabilise the Labour Governments of the 1960s and 1970s. The British government's abortive attempts to ban the publication of *Spycatcher* ultimately led to the ridiculous spectacle of Sir Robert Armstrong, the Head of the Civil Service, appearing in an Australian court in 1987 to argue the case of his political masters. In taking this action, Armstrong seemed to be only too willing to follow the inexorable logic of his own Memorandum (the civil servant's sole loyalty lies with the government of the day), but his unquestioning defence of secrecy in this case caused concern within and beyond the civil service.

The cumulative effect of the Tisdall, Ponting and *Spycatcher* affairs was to propel the government into consideration of reform of the

Official Secrets Acts. The result was the 1989 Official Secrets Act, which was a liberalising measure in some respects, but did not in any sense fulfil the expectations of the proponents of open government.

The Act removed the great mass of official information from the 'secret' category, while protecting most of it from disclosure by bringing it within the ambit of the CSPCS Code (from 1993, the Civil Service Management Code, within which the Armstrong Memorandum was enshrined). Hence, the disclosure of information about many domestic issues, such as social or economic policy, would no longer be covered by the criminal law, but would still carry the threat of sanctions (up to and including dismissal from the service) under the Code.

The information still covered by the Act itself was divided into five categories, each of which contained criminal sanctions against disclosure. Thus, disclosure of security and intelligence information was an absolute offence, regardless of harm done, while disclosure of information in the four other categories (defence, international relations, information received in confidence from foreign governments or international organisations, and information of use to criminals) would result in conviction if it could be shown that harm had been done by the disclosure.

The 1989 Act created a new offence: publication of leaked documents. Furthermore, it closed the loophole on the 'public interest defence'. Juries were to be offered no scope to ponder whether a disclosure aimed to publicise unconstitutional, illegal or politically contentious issues: the prosecution had only to show that 'harm' had been done by the disclosure to secure conviction.

The hopes of reformers had effectively been dashed. This was no 'whistle-blower's charter'. The Tisdall and Ponting prosecutions would still have been possible under this legislation, with two extra features: in the Tisdall case, *The Guardian* would also have been liable to prosecution for publishing stories based on a leaked document which fell within one of the categories of classified information; in the Ponting case, there would have been no recourse to a 'public interest/interest of the state' defence.

Major's initiatives

After the 1992 General Election, the Major Government appeared to be keen to tackle at least some aspects of the culture of secrecy.

Within a relatively short period the government sanctioned publication of the membership of Cabinet committees, and the official rule book for ministerial conduct, *Questions of Procedure for Ministers* (Cabinet Office, 1992) was released. This was the type of information which informed journalists had managed to publicise in the past, but now, at last, the government was opening up on its own initiative.

More significant developments were to come. In July 1993, the government took the unprecedented step of publishing a brochure on the organisation of MI5, the security service (HMSO, 1993a), in which the Director-General, Stella Rimington, was openly identified. Three months later, similar information was released about the intelligence services (HMSO, 1993b), and in March 1994 the forthcoming replacement of Sir Colin McColl as 'C' (the head of MI6) by David Spedding, was given considerable publicity. None the less, the government blocked attempts to give Parliament a role in scrutinising the security and intelligence services.

After a delay of some months, said to be caused by internal Whitehall disputes, the government published a White Paper on open government in July 1993 (White Paper, 1993). This represented a genuine, but very limited, incremental step in the direction of greater openness. Judged against the standards of the United States of America and other states, the White Paper scarcely represented 'open government' at all, but judged against the traditions of British government, this was a progressive measure. The open government White Paper contained a Code of Practice on Government Information, which came into force in April 1994. Under the Code, the government was committed to do the following:

- Publish the key background facts and analysis along with major policy pronouncements.
- Make available explanatory material on departmental dealings with the public.
- Give reasons for administrative decisions affecting individuals or organisations.
- Supply, on request, further information relating to departmental activities, although a charge could be made for this service.

- Publish information about public services in accordance with
the Citizen's Charter, including information on costs, standards, performance and complaints and redress procedures.

Information which, in the government's view, could affect defence
or national security, assist criminal activities, hinder the operations
of the public service, infringe the privacy of the Royal household
or damage the commercial interests of companies would not be
released. The Code of Practice was to be monitored by the Parliamentary Commissioner for Administration, who would have the
power to investigate complaints from members of the public
(channelled through MPs) about the alleged failure of public
bodies to meet their responsibilities under the Code.

Additionally, the White Paper contained a commitment to introduce statutory rights of access to personal records and to health
and safety information. However, this was the sole legislative reference in the White Paper: access to the other types of information
would remain at the discretion of ministers, on the advice of their
officials. There was no legal 'right to know'. Furthermore, the
government was keen to stress that it was proposing to widen
access to 'information', as distinct from documents.

The White Paper committed the government to review the numerous legislative provisions (including the 1989 Official Secrets
Act) which prohibit the disclosure of information, but there were
no indications that a 'whistle-blower's charter' was on the way.
What seemed to be envisaged was a marginal relaxation of sanctions in cases where very low-grade, non-confidential information
is disclosed.

It may take the experience of a number of years before the true
impact of this initiative becomes clear. Analysts and commentators
tended to welcome the White Paper with two cheers, at best. The
comments of Patrick Birkinshaw were typical:

> The White Paper's commitment to, and promise of, greater open-
> ness is to be welcomed. There can be little doubt that modest
> though many of the proposals are, they will be viewed as a sea
> change in many parts of Whitehall and they may well be responsible
> for promoting a change in culture. . . . But . . . it maintains an an-
> cient tradition that the business of government . . . is not for the
> people as of right. Not even on terms that have been accepted
> through much of the English-speaking common law world, including

those countries built upon the Westminster style of government. That makes the White Paper remarkable: indeed, it would be viewed in many of those countries as risible. (Birkinshaw, 1993: 568)

Clouding out the sun

At around the same time as the government was publishing its White Paper on open government, and allowing a few beams of sunlight to illuminate certain limited areas of government activity, there was a clear illustration of how the clouds of secrecy could block out the sun. The 'Arms for Iraq' affair raised a whole series of questions about the conduct of official business and the flow of information between Whitehall and Parliament.

Following the collapse of what became known as the Matrix Churchill trial in November 1992, the government established an independent judicial inquiry under Lord Justice Scott to investigate the circumstances surrounding the supply of military and military-related equipment to Iraq. In particular, the inquiry would focus on the question of whether the government had breached its own ban on arms sales to Iraq, and on the conduct of ministers and civil servants in relation to the prosecution of three company executives from the machine tools firm, Matrix Churchill (Leigh, 1993).

As ministers and civil servants gave evidence in public to the Scott inquiry, the culture of secrecy was thoroughly exposed. Five ministers had signed Public Interest Immunity Certificates in order to suppress information about government knowledge of the true nature of export contracts, thus effectively jeopardising the liberty of the Matrix Churchill defendants. Ministers had also misled Parliament about the shift of policy in relation to defence sales to Iraq. Civil servants had undoubtedly been implicated in these, and other dubious actions in the course of the whole affair. It appeared that none of the officials involved in these acts of collusion seemed to question the ethics of the matter. Perhaps the ethos of the Armstrong Memorandum had seeped into the soul of the civil servants implicated in the Matrix Churchill affair.

It almost added insult to an injured reputation when, in his evidence to the Scott inquiry in February 1994, Sir Robin Butler, the Head of the Civil Service, defended ministerial statements to Parliament, on the rather questionable grounds that 'half the picture can be true' (Butler, 1994a: 54). As a justification of the culture of secrecy, this surely ranked with the immortal words of Butler's predecessor, Sir Robert Armstrong. In the Australian courtroom, while propping up the British government's attempt to ban publication of *Spycatcher*, Armstrong had equated official lies with being 'economical with the truth'.

In this chapter, we have seen that the British civil service operates within a prevailing climate of official secrecy. The fundamental reasons for this have been explained, and the ramifications of secrecy in government outlined. The ethical dilemmas and crises of conscience which have confronted civil servants as individuals, and the civil service as an organisation have been examined. The catalytic effect of the Tisdall and Ponting cases brought responses of sorts from the government, but, progress in this realm appears to be characterised by crab-like steps, rather than purposeful strides.

8

WHITEHALL AND BRUSSELS

Membership of the European Union (as the European Community was formally restyled in November 1993) has had a significant impact upon British government and politics. In the period since the United Kingdom joined the EC in 1973, the civil service has been charged with an increasing range of responsibilities related to European policy-making and implementation. While retaining its traditional practices and characteristics in relation to the European facets of its work, the civil service has also adjusted and adapted itself to the requirements of membership.

In the past it has been possible for the authors of texts on the civil service to make do with the odd passing reference to 'the European dimension'. Implicitly or explicitly, this is often portrayed as rather dull and unexciting. To some extent, this is understandable: Peter Hennessy cites Harold Macmillan's attempts to convince his unenthusiastic colleagues that Europe 'isn't just about fixing a price for prunes and a suitable method of marketing bananas' (Hennessy, 1989a: 253). However, the importance of the European Union for the British polity cannot be denied. Now, over twenty years since the date of accession, with the sheer volume of European work steadily mounting, those seeking to explain and understand the British civil service can no longer be satisfied with fleeting references to Whitehall and Brussels.

Britain and the development of the European Union

In order to approach a proper understanding of the civil service's role in relation to the European Union, and to place the official work in a broader context, it is important for us to establish some basic points about the emergence of the EU, and Britain's ambivalent approach to European integration. The particular nature of the challenges facing the British civil service in relation to the EU can only be grasped if we remind ourselves of the circuitous route Britain took to membership, and the mantle of the 'reluctant European' with which it has been clothed ever since.

British isolationism

During the formative period of western European economic co-operation, from the late 1940s until the early 1960s, British governments remained on the sidelines, viewing developments with a mixture of scepticism and disinterest (George, 1990: Chapter 1).

Although Britain participated in the US-funded European Recovery Programme ('Marshall Aid') from 1948, it did not view the Programme's co-ordinating body, the Organisation for European Economic Cooperation, as the precursor of full-blooded economic unity. Other governments, and key individuals including the senior French civil servant Jean Monnet and the French Foreign Minister Robert Schuman, took a different view. In 1951, agreement was reached between France, West Germany, Italy, Belgium, Luxembourg and the Netherlands regarding the establishment of the European Coal and Steel Community (ECSC).

After a series of disappointments for the federalists who saw the ECSC as the launching pad for 'sectoral integration' and favoured a speedy move towards substantial economic, military and political unity, a widening of the common market beyond coal and steel was eventually proposed at the Messina Conference in 1955. Following detailed negotiations, during the initial stages of which Britain was represented at official (but not political) level, treaties were signed by the six member states of the ECSC in Rome in March 1957. The treaties set up the European Atomic Energy Community ('Euratom') to facilitate the peaceful development of atomic power, and the European Economic Community (EEC), which provided for the removal of internal tariff barriers, the creation of common external tariffs and the abolition of obstacles to the free movement of people and capital. Britain's suspicions about the political consequences of the drive for European economic unity were apparently confirmed in the wording of the Treaty of Rome:

> While ostensibly about economics, the preamble of the EEC Treaty made it clear that the objective was 'to lay the foundation of an ever closer union amongst the peoples of Europe'. What had been embarked upon was both an economic and a political exercise. (George, 1991: 11)

In July 1967 the ECSC, Euratom and the EEC were formally merged to form the European Community.

Why did the British governments, both Labour and Conservative, choose to remain aloof from the events leading up to the establishment of these European institutions? A distinct distrust of economic and political federalism, already alluded to, was clearly one factor. For Britain, unlike the six founding members, the validity of the independent nation state had been confirmed by her wartime experience. Ultimately undefeated, and unoccupied, Britain and its governments seemed to lack the more relaxed and questioning approach adopted by some of the west European states towards matters of national sovereignty (although this point should not be over-emphasised, since France tended to adopt a strong line on matters pertaining to sovereignty and its national interest when this was convenient). Beyond this, Britain's modern historical role in continental Europe had been as the arbiter of disputes, and this would have to be sacrificed if it were to become a full participant in internal European affairs. In addition to these rather general factors, matters of *realpolitik* contributed to the British stance.

Britain's status as a major power, with a place on the Security Council of the United Nations, and possessing the atomic bomb, seemed to most domestic politicians to place it in a different league from 'the Six'. Associated with this point, the traditional concept of 'three circles of influence' in British foreign policy (the Atlantic alliance, the Empire/Commonwealth and Europe) dictated an approach which placed western European concerns within a broader perspective.

Finally, at least until the late 1950s, key groups within the major parties of government in Britain adopted what was, at best, an ambivalent attitude towards the idea of European co-operation. In the Labour Party, there were concerns that the democratic socialist advances made in the period 1945–51 could be sacrificed if Britain was sucked into an enterprise which seemed to be primarily designed to advance the interests of western European business. In the Conservative Party, the doubts were mainly associated with the possible sacrifice of sovereignty to a supra-national organisation, together with a lingering attachment to Empire.

The reluctant European comes in from the cold

A series of factors combined to bring about a fundamental change in the attitude of British governments towards European economic co-operation. Firstly, by the late 1950s and early 1960s Britain's economic performance was beginning to appear distinctly sluggish in comparison with that of the leading participants in the EEC (in particular, West Germany, where an 'economic miracle' had transformed the state). At a time when the fastest growth in trade was between industrialised states, Britain had limited access to the markets of western Europe.

Secondly, it had become clear that the EEC was not going to collapse in disarray, contrary to the expectations of at least some British sceptics. The Six were making a success of their experiment.

Thirdly, as the Empire metamorphosed into the Commonwealth, Britain gradually lost the extremely favourable terms of trade which are the prerogative of an imperial power, and had to negotiate new, less favourable terms, with the independent states. In a broader sense too, the Commonwealth proved to be less amenable to Britain, as was illustrated by the decision to expel South Africa in 1961 against the wishes of the British government.

Fourthly, with the advent of the Kennedy presidency in January 1961, Britain's closest and most powerful ally began to give positive encouragement to British participation in the EEC (partly for selfish American concerns, it should be added!).

Finally, enthusiasts for European co-operation and those who were neutral on this issue began to move into the ascendancy in both the Conservative and Labour Parties as the new decade began (although it should be noted that they were not unchallenged, and Labour's leader until 1963, Hugh Gaitskell, remained implacably opposed to British membership of the EEC).

Thus, the Government of Harold Macmillan formally applied for membership of the EEC in 1961, and detailed negotiations were conducted during the next two years, only to end with the imposition of a French veto in January 1963. This stemmed in large measure from President Charles de Gaulle's hostility to US involvement in the affairs of western Europe: an involvement he believed would be intensified should Washington's close ally join the EEC. The Labour Government of Harold Wilson launched the second bid for membership, only to receive a similar rebuff in 1967.

With de Gaulle no longer in office, Edward Heath's Conservative Government filed Britain's third application in 1971, and, following negotiation over the terms of entry, Heath signed the Treaty of Rome in January 1972. Britain formally joined the EC a year later.

A member of what? The key European institutions

On becoming a member, the British government, through its ministers and civil servants, began to participate in the complex process of European policy-making and implementation which is now centred on five key institutions.

The first of these, the European Council, consists of the heads of government of the member states, together with the President of the Commission (see below), and generally meets twice a year in order to give an overall direction to the work of the EU and resolve any particularly intractable disputes.

The second key institution is the Council of Ministers, which effectively acts as the decision-making executive of the European Union. It takes different forms according to the subjects under discussion at any given time, and can consequently be a Council of foreign ministers, trade ministers, agriculture ministers, environment ministers or whatever. The presidency of the Council rotates among the member states every six months, and the relevant ministers from the presiding state will chair all the meetings of the Council and seek to achieve particular objectives during this period.

Depending on the subject under discussion, the Council of Ministers takes decisions by unanimous agreement, qualified majority voting (which gives a weighting to the votes of the member states) or simple majority. European law is adopted in three forms: 'Regulations', which are binding on member governments and the citizens of member states; 'Decisions', which are binding on those to whom they are addressed; and 'Directives', which are binding in terms of the result to be achieved, but national governments are allowed to find the most appropriate form of implementation (for example, legislation or statutory instrument).

The Council of Ministers has its own structure of official support, the Committee of Permanent Representatives, or COREPER. This is split into two elements: COREPER I supports the foreign ministers of the member states, and consists of the national ambassadors to the EU, while COREPER II supports the other ministers, and consists of a range of appropriately skilled national civil servants. British civil servants working within COREPER are based within the United Kingdom's Permanent Representation, are known collectively as UKREP, and have been described as Whitehall's 'hidden arm in Brussels' (Young and Sloman, 1982: 73). The Committee of Permanent Representatives does not normally deal with agricultural policy. The Common Agricultural Policy (CAP) is the responsibility of the Special Committee on Agriculture (SCA), which has the same status as COREPER, and is composed of senior officials from the Permanent Representatives or from the agriculture ministries of the member states.

The Commission, the third key institution, is charged with the tasks of proposing new EU policies and laws for consideration by the Council of Ministers, and then ensuring that these are properly implemented. The governments of the larger member states, including Britain, appoint two Commissioners each, while the smaller states appoint one each. The Commissioners are allocated particular policy portfolios, head directorates which are staffed by supporting bureaucracies and have their work co-ordinated by the President of the Commission. Although vested with an authority that is independent of the member governments, the Commission is also obliged to work closely with, and is tied by the decisions of, the Council of Ministers.

The fourth body, the European Parliament, is directly elected every five years. Seats are distributed between the member states according to size of population. It has a range of formal advisory and supervisory powers, but has lacked the clout of a true 'parliament', at least until the coming of the Single European Act and the Maastricht Treaty. Its main role has been to agree the budget for the EU (along with the Council of Ministers), to approve the appointment of the Commission, to give its opinion on proposals coming before the Commission and the Council and to ratify international agreements entered into by the EU. Reforms introduced through the mechanisms of the Single European Act and Maastricht have strengthened the role of the European Parliament in the legislative process, to the point where it is effectively a joint legislature (with the Council of Ministers) in some policy spheres.

Finally, the European Court of Justice is charged with interpreting EU treaties, judging contraventions of European law, and fining those who fail to comply with its judgements. Member states, other EU institutions, individuals, national courts and companies all have the right of appeal to the Court of Justice.

The 'awkward partner'

Two general factors contributed to many of the problems Britain would encounter within the European Community/Union, leading to her image as 'an awkward partner' (George, 1990). Britain had belatedly joined an organisation which had been moulded by the original six members in their own interests. Moreover, this organisation had partly been founded on the principle of creating an 'ever closer union' in political as well as economic terms. This principle aroused much suspicion even on the part of some British politicians who were enthusiastic about economic co-operation.

It is not difficult to find evidence of Britain's propensity for challenging European norms:

- Britain's terms of entry were renegotiated following the return of the Labour Government in 1974, and a referendum was required the following year before continued membership could be assured.
- In Britain, the introduction of direct elections to the European Parliament was delayed until 1979.
- Britain refused to join the European Monetary System in 1978–9.
- There were protracted rows over Britain's budgetary contributions between 1979 and 1984.

- Britain hindered movement towards the introduction of a single European currency, and refused to participate in key steps towards achieving this by 1999.
- At the 1991 Maastricht summit, Britain opted out of the 'Social Chapter', which would have widened the common employment and social policies of the member states.
- Having belatedly taken sterling into the Exchange Rate Mechanism, Britain left the ERM in the wake of 'Black Wednesday' in September 1992.
- A recurring theme of British policy within the EU has been to put a brake on moves towards the ultimate creation of a federal Europe. This was exemplified by the British government's insistence that the word 'federal' be removed from the Maastricht Treaty.

Too much can be made of these, and other, examples: after all, Britain is not unique in attempting to defend what it perceives to be its national interest or the long-term interest of the EU, and, in some cases, it has received sympathy and support from other member states. None the less, it is important for us to grasp the general climate within which the British civil service has operated as the official arm of what was generally perceived to be Europe's 'awkward partner' since 1973.

How Whitehall links up with the European network

The interconnections between the British civil service and the European Union are complex and sophisticated. The arrangements for official linkages with the EU are characterised by a fair degree of fragmentation. While adopting a focus on institutions and departments has its limitations, by far the simplest approach to understanding the links between Whitehall and Brussels is to set out the roles and responsibilities of the key co-ordinating bodies.

While doing this, we should bear in mind the broad parameters within which the civil service is operating in this context. Two of the fundamental civil service roles of policy advice and policy execution or implementation, to which we have referred throughout this book, have a particular application here.

Officials involved in EU work, at various levels both domestically and in Brussels, can be seen as offering policy advice to their ministers in order to facilitate effective ministerial inputs into (and relationships with) the European Council and the Council of Ministers. There has been some debate about the extent to which the particular nature of their work has allowed civil servants based within UKREP to stray over the invisible line dividing policy advice and policy creation: we shall return to this issue in due course.

The second basic civil service role which looms large in the European context is that of policy implementation. Decisions emanating from the Commission and the Court of Justice must be effectively executed.

At this point, it is worth returning to the comment made in the early part of this chapter, and noting that the very nature of civil service work in relation to Europe can be affected by the attitude of government, and particular ministers, to the EU. In the performance of their advisory and implementation roles, officials may be operating in an environment which is of special political concern to their ministerial masters. Civil servants dealing with European matters in the period 1979–90 could hardly be in any doubt about the attitude of the Prime Minister towards Brussels. In a more specific sense, officials working in departments headed by avowed 'Euro-sceptics' such as Tony Benn in the 1970s, Nicholas Ridley, Peter Lilley or Michael Portillo, may find the high political saliency of their advisory or implementation tasks is either a liberating or a constraining factor, depending on the circumstances!

In relation to each of these spheres of work, civil servants perform a major co-ordinating function, drawing together the various component parts of British policy and administration which have a European dimension.

Thus, in simple terms, we can say that the British civil service has a dual responsibility: helping to feed policy inputs into the EU machine, and securing effective implementation of the outputs being churned out by Brussels. This has been achieved in a manner typical of the civil service: through the development of new bodies, especially UKREP in Brussels, which operate within a traditional constitutional framework; and through the steady evolution of extant bodies, including the Cabinet Office, the Foreign and Commonwealth Office and other departments of state.

Despite the fact that membership of the European Union has brought the civil service into close contact with national and EU administrative systems which have quite different characteristics, traditions and procedures from the British model, it has adjusted to the demands of membership remarkably well.

> British arrangements for the co-ordination of European policy are generally reckoned to be the most effective of any of the Member States. . . . The British pride themselves on their regular high score on the European Commission's own table of punctual implementation of Community legislation. (Spence, 1993: 53)

Let us now try to shed further light on the European dimensions of civil service work by examining the part played by officials in a range of key bodies.

The Foreign and Commonwealth Office (FCO)

Although the Diplomatic Service is distinct from the Home Civil Service, and is not the prime concern of this book, it is impossible to comprehend the official links between Britain and the EU, or to view the part played by civil servants in proper perspective, without giving some consideration to the FCO.

In a general sense, Britain's membership of the European Union increased the involvement of the FCO in the work of domestic departments of state, and brought about closer working relations between the Diplomatic Service and the Home Civil Service. For some observers, and participants, this has been a matter of concern. Tony Benn's view is clear:

> I think the Foreign Office influence on Whitehall is now quite pernicious because the Foreign Office can properly claim that every bit of economic policy, industrial policy, social policy, is now European policy and has to be fed through them. If they think it will interfere with our relations with our partners in the Community they will veto it, if they can, in Whitehall. If it isn't vetoed in Whitehall, they will be party to the process by which the Brussels Commission might veto it. And that is a fundamental change in allegiance. (Young and Sloman, 1982: 80)

Benn's view has been echoed by one of his colleagues in the Labour Governments of the 1970s, Roy Hattersley, who, although markedly more pro-European than Benn, has spoken of Foreign

Office officials 'interfering in agricultural prices; they're interfering in economic policy; they're interfering in energy policy' (Young and Sloman, 1982: 81). Frustrated by what she perceived to be an over-close allegiance to Brussels, and a malign influence over domestic policy, Margaret Thatcher once considered stripping the FCO of its responsibility for European matters, and creating a new department for European affairs (Hennessy, 1989a: 405).

It is important, however, to place these views of FCO 'empire-building' in perspective. In the period leading up to Britain's accession to the EC in 1973, the FCO naturally took a leading role in the negotiations. Thereafter, a tension developed between the traditional FCO perspective that Europe was a legitimate sphere of foreign policy within which the Foreign Office should continue to play the leading role, and an alternative view, epitomised by Edward Heath, which saw membership not in terms of participation in a 'foreign body', but as a new dimension of domestic government and politics (Salmon, 1995). This tension undoubtedly contributed to the frustration and annoyance of Benn, Hattersley and others, and still re-emerges from time to time. None the less, as we shall see, it seems clear that the FCO has gradually been obliged to cede elements of its central co-ordinating role to the Cabinet Office, and faces increasing practical challenges to its role as the primary channel of communication between Whitehall departments and the EU.

What is the role of the FCO in relation to Europe, and how do its officials work with their counterparts in the Home Civil Service? The logistics of FCO European business are relatively straightforward. Two functional departments within the Foreign Office have responsibility for overseeing the full range of EU matters, co-ordinating the work of UKREP in Brussels and providing the government with policy briefing and negotiating expertise. Specifically, the European Community Department (Internal) has a role in monitoring and contributing to EU aspects of domestic policy-making, including the development of the single market, while the European Community Department (External) focuses on the broader strategic issues such as European Political Co-operation (the move towards an ever closer political union) and the EU's external relations.

The FCO is formally charged with receiving and distributing all EU material, including reports and proposals from the Commission, and communications regarding each day's business in

Brussels. In addition, information is transmitted by the FCO to UKREP on behalf of other government departments, although the use of fax machines and the development of departmental expertise in co-ordinating their own EU business has resulted in the increased by-passing of the FCO by civil servants in other departments (Spence, 1993: 61). Furthermore, although they are formally accountable to the FCO, civil servants seconded from home departments to work in UKREP maintain close links with their colleagues in Whitehall.

It is possible that the role of the FCO in relation to EU matters might decline in time. The rationale for the European Departments of the Foreign Office has been questioned (Spence, 1993: 63), on the ground that the home departments have taken on increasing responsibility for European business (and jealously guard their status as 'lead departments' in certain spheres). Furthermore, the Cabinet Office performs a useful co-ordination function, and the whole issue of European relations appears less and less distinct as a matter of 'foreign policy'.

UK Permanent Representation in Brussels

In formal terms, UKREP is an overseas post of the Foreign and Commonwealth Office. However, although the forty or so senior officials within UKREP are headed by the Permanent Representative, who is a career diplomat of senior ambassadorial status, approximately two-thirds of them are civil servants from other Whitehall departments, normally on secondment for two-year periods. In addition, the deputy to the Permanent Representative is usually a senior civil servant from the Department of Trade and Industry (Spence, 1993: 64). 'In its own way, the Permanent Representation is a mini-Whitehall, and is thus quite different from the usual British embassy abroad' (Kirchner, 1993: 183). David Spence has identified three general functions performed by the officials in UKREP (Spence, 1993: 63–8):

● Provision of an advisory, information and co-ordinating facility for all Whitehall negotiators coming to Brussels.

● Monitoring developments in the EU institutions on behalf of the British government. In this capacity, UKREP officials participate in the work of the satellite groups surrounding the Council of Ministers, and operate as lobbyists for Britain with the Commission and the European Parliament. Early warning of forthcoming developments is channelled back to Whitehall by the UKREP officials, and the Permanent Representative will attend meetings in the Cabinet Office on a weekly basis.

- Negotiating in the working groups linked to the Council of Ministers. While fulfilling this function, the UKREP officials rely heavily upon briefings provided by the relevant Whitehall departments, and they will often be joined by colleagues from these departments when negotiations enter highly technical areas. UKREP has a formal responsibility to provide the FCO with daily summaries of the negotiations taking place in the working groups, and these are then used to brief senior civil servants in Whitehall.

The civil servants working within UKREP are the only British representatives permanently based in Brussels (since the two Commissioners are not, strictly speaking, 'representing' British interests). Additionally, they operate with a considerable degree of freedom when negotiating on Britain's behalf within the labyrinthine groups and committees linked to the Council of Ministers. This raises an important question about the impact of Brussels on the civil service:

> Is it a place where, because of distance and because there are so many decisions to be taken, the lines of distinction between decisions taken properly by politicians and those taken improperly by officials have become blurred? (Young and Sloman, 1982: 76)

Upon asking this question, Hugo Young and Anne Sloman were deluged with protestations from civil servants, who described the official environment of Brussels as layer upon layer of committees, replete with complex arrangements for reporting back to ministers. Far from serving to free civil servants from political control, this simply yoked them tightly to their political masters (Young and Sloman, 1982: 77–81). One might conclude that they 'protest too much'. However, having taken time to study the work of both civil servants and ministers at close quarters in Brussels, Young and Sloman concluded that:

Brussels is not a mandarin's playground in the sense of letting civil servants off the leash of the constitution and giving them enormous untrammelled power. On the contrary, the opposite is truer: that in this area of government activity, as in few others, the lines of political control are drawn tight. (Young and Sloman, 1982: 79)

The Cabinet Office

As Britain joined the EC, there was a general suspicion on the part of key figures in other departments that the FCO was unlikely to have either the inclination or the detailed knowledge required to defend British interests in Europe. Furthermore, the FCO had a particular departmental view on European issues, and it was felt that this might occasionally be incompatible with its role as an arbiter in Whitehall disputes about such issues. Accordingly, the Cabinet Office, as a body with no particular policy axes of its own to grind, came to be allocated a share in the European co-ordinating function.

The European Secretariat of the Cabinet Office is a relatively small body, with a staff of only around twenty civil servants, who, like the other Cabinet Office officials, are on secondment from other Whitehall departments. None the less, it convenes approximately 200 inter-departmental meetings of civil servants every year, including the weekly meeting attended by the Permanent Representative (Nugent, 1993: 55), and annually circulates over 300 papers (Bender, 1991: 16). In addition, the European Secretariat provides a high-level secretarial support system for Cabinet meetings at which EU issues are discussed, as well as for meetings of the key Cabinet committees which handle European matters (the Overseas and Defence Committee, its Sub-committee on Overseas and Defence (Europe), the European Questions (Steering) Committee and the European Questions (Official) Committee).

The basic functions of the European Secretariat have been described by David Spence (1993: 55-7) as follows:

- Managing the European items on the agenda of the Cabinet and Cabinet committees.
- Co-ordinating and chairing inter-departmental meetings of officials on European issues.
- Providing authoritative guidance for departmental civil servants on EU issues pertaining to British policy.

- Monitoring the process of parliamentary scrutiny. This involves ensuring that government departments are acting properly with respect to the work of the Commons and Lords committees charged with scrutinising EU business.
- Monitoring all EU legislation, to ensure that implementation deadlines are adhered to and legal proceedings involving Britain are being conducted satisfactorily.

Departments and agencies

For some government departments, such as the Ministry of Agriculture, Fisheries and Food (MAFF), the Department of Trade and Industry (DTI) and the Treasury, Europe loomed large from the day of Britain's accession, if not before. Together with their colleagues in the Cabinet Office, the FCO and UKREP, civil servants in these departments formed an early version of what Michael Clarke has described as an elite 'Euro-mafia' (1990: 27). Quite simply, these domestic departments entered the European orbit because of the fundamental importance of, respectively, the Common Agricultural Policy, the panoply of European trading regulations and directives and the centrality of expenditure issues in virtually every sphere of European policy. One measure of the significance of the EU for such departments is the human traffic which flows between them and Brussels: it has been estimated that MAFF alone sends, on average, 200 officials each month to meetings there (Young and Sloman, 1982: 73).

However, as the areas of competence ceded to Brussels have expanded, so more and more departments have been pulled into this orbit.

> Departments which might have been regarded as very much domestically-oriented, e.g. the Home Office or the Department of Health, have assumed responsibility for the handling of Community negotiations on particular issues. Related to this is the fact that very few if any current EC issues are of concern only to one government department: most involve several departments. (Bender, 1991: 14)

Bender might have added to his list the name of almost any Whitehall department. Most will have to assume the 'lead role' in relation to one or other aspect of EU policy at any given time, and, as Bender notes, play a contributory part in relation to other

European matters. Furthermore, responsibility for implementing EU policy in certain spheres has now passed to Next Steps executive agencies. For example, the Intervention Board is charged with the task of implementing the British components of the Common Agricultural Policy.

A distinct pattern has emerged within departments for dealing with this growing weight of EU business. Initially, European elements of policy can be handled by the department's international division, but then, as the volume of work increases, a European division is established. This tends to steer clear of highly technical negotiations, consultations with key interest groups, or detailed matters of implementation (which are left to the civil servants working in the relevant functional divisions of the department), but concentrates on co-ordinating the department's overall approach to the EU (Spence, 1993: 62), and general liaison with other departments, the FCO, the Cabinet Office and UKREP.

Membership of the EU has transformed the organisational ethos of some departments of state, and has had a concomitant effect on the working lives of many civil servants. The praise heaped upon MAFF officials by Peter Walker when he was Minister for Agriculture exemplifies this point:

> It is quite a tribute to the civil service that a department which was, I suppose, the most inward-looking and domestically-oriented department in Whitehall until we joined the Community, now probably has the best negotiating team (I'm talking about officials, no flattery to the ministers) in Brussels of any member country. (Young and Sloman, 1982: 74)

Departments are keen to preserve as much scope as possible for independent action within their own areas of competence. They tend to emphasise the more technical aspects of the European work which comes their way, while stressing their own unique expertise and capacity to deal with these matters. Civil servants have had to become adept at winning 'turf battles' in order to win or preserve their department's status as the 'lead' in given spheres of EU policy.

Having emphasised the growing importance of the European Union to the work of the British civil service, we are left with one final question: to what extent are officials specifically trained for this type of activity?

Grooming the Eurocrats

To a certain extent, many of the techniques and skills associated with the European elements of civil service work are identical to those required for other types of work. However, the high premium placed upon lobbying and negotiating, both with Brussels and within Whitehall, together with the inherent complexity of the EU decision-making process, would ostensibly seem to create a demand for a newer breed of official. The 'Euro-literate' civil servant might be developed through specific training programmes offered to those likely to encounter the EU dimension in the course of their work (an increasing number), or he or she might be recruited directly.

Given this point, it is something of a surprise to note that there was a relative paucity of schemes and programmes designed to engender this new breed, at least until 1994, when the number and the profile of such schemes was partially raised.

As far as the training aspect is concerned, departments and agencies have opportunities to send their officials to occasional courses on specific aspects of EU work, run by the Civil Service College. However, as late as 1993, the College seemed to place considerably more emphasis on its co-ordinated 'market testing' courses than on the European ones, and the observer was left with the impression that whatever specific 'EU training' existed was carried out predominantly in-house, by departments and agencies themselves. European training was identified as a growth area of College business, and a marked expansion took place in this area in 1994–5 (Civil Service College, 1994). The College offered a four-stage 'European Competence Programme', short 'Framework Courses', 'Skills Courses' (including how to deal with EU Directives, and how to negotiate in EU meetings), policy briefings on specific topics, as well as courses of guidance on European law and economics. In addition, the College collaborated with the Cabinet Office to offer an intensive package of training for entrants to the European Fast Stream.

This fast stream was introduced in 1990, as part of the overall civil service fast-stream recruitment programme (Civil Service Commissioners, 1991: 8; Recruitment and Assessment Services, 1993). However, the European Fast Stream is primarily designed to increase the number of UK nationals working within the EU institutions. Under the scheme, up to thirty young lawyers, economists and administrators are taken into the civil service and placed in the Cabinet Office. From there, they are seconded to other government departments to be given relevant European work experience. In addition, they are given extensive training in preparation for the highly competitive EU recruitment schemes. Those who succeed leave the British civil service and join one of the EU institutions. Applicants who fail in the EU schemes are given the option of remaining in the civil service.

No published figures or analysis of this scheme are available as yet. Accordingly, it is not possible to comment on the success rate of the British candidates, or on the extent to which unsuccessful candidates have been allocated to posts with a strong European dimension in home departments (which would seem to make some kind of sense, given the nature of their induction to the civil service).

The generally favourable impression of the British civil service's European capacity, conveyed earlier, perhaps indicates that the tendency for a relatively low profile to be accorded to EU training and recruitment has done no damage to date. However, one only has to consider the steadily growing significance of the European Union to the work of the civil service in order to appreciate that complacency in this sphere would be distinctly inappropriate.

The apparent federalisation of the civil service, a theme which has recurred in various guises throughout this book, can be discerned once again, in the context of the EU dimension of civil service work. The secondment of officials to UKREP, and the creation of what Kirchner described as 'a mini-Whitehall' in Brussels, is one element of this. Here, there is physical, structural detachment of parts of the civil service from the parent departments, albeit with elaborate arrangements for communication and liaison with the real Whitehall. Another aspect of federalisation is more subtle. The growing European divisions within departments of state and executive agencies arguably present us with a strain of federalism which cuts across some of those we have already identified. As the weight of European work (both the policy advice and the implementation aspects) steadily increases, its impact on the civil service can hardly fail to be significant.

As we are now beginning to touch upon broader issues relating to the future of the civil service, it would be appropriate to develop the theme further, in our concluding chapter.

9

CONCLUSION
Still one civil service?

At virtually every stage of our examination of the civil service, we have encountered a recurring theme. The most significant structural and managerial developments of the 1980s and 1990s have involved decentralisation, delegation and devolution. The cumulative effect of these has been to produce a movement away from the traditional, centralised and unitary civil service towards what we have described as a federation.

The Next Steps initiative, and the proliferation of executive agencies which it spawned, is but the most obvious example of this trend. When the increasing delegation of managerial powers over budgets, recruitment, training, pay and conditions of service is considered, and once the self-imposed weakening of the Treasury/Cabinet Office grip over the minutiae of civil service affairs enters the equation, we can perhaps discern the shape of things to come. A much looser federation of reasonably discrete organisational entities, each with its own ethos and sub-culture, seems to be gradually taking the place of the old monolith. One close observer of the Next Steps initiative has predicted that within the smaller and more diverse civil service of the future, the very term 'civil servant' will become 'increasingly meaningless'. Government employees will be more likely to identify with their particular agency or department than with a huge organisation (Greer, 1994: 103). Warren Fisher must be turning in his grave!

Do the sweeping and detailed reforms which have been introduced across the civil service, mainly in the period since 1979, represent a simple acceleration of the evolutionary process, or has there been a radical break with the traditions of the British civil service, to the extent that it is effectively disintegrating? Can the civil service still stand as a cohesive entity, or is it being 'Balkanised', broken up into increasingly independent component parts? Has the move from the unitary civil service gone beyond the federal stage, to the point where there is no longer *one* civil service?

Some observers fear that the point of no return may already have been reached. Richard Chapman encapsulates such a view:

> the British civil service, as a distinct institution of the public service, identifiable primarily through certain characteristics or qualities . . . no longer exists. If others claim that it does, can they reasonably point to unifying characteristics to sustain that claim? How can such an institution be so identified if it has flexible methods of selection of staff; or has different staff grading and pay structures; or different conditions of service for staff employed in a large number of independent or quasi-independent departments and agencies? . . . Moreover, throughout the system, if system it is, there is positive encouragement of staff to identify with their independent units rather than with the service as a whole; and there is encouragement too, for staff to discard their anonymity and exercise management enterprise and initiative on their own account. (Chapman, 1992: 4)

With the possible exception of a small band of political zealots within the 'New Right', there is a general recognition, across the political spectrum, that if Chapman's vision of a disintegrating civil service is accurate, the British system of government will be the loser. Is his vision accurate?

Before addressing this question directly, we should put the civil service reforms of the 1980s and 1990s into perspective. This period has certainly been characterised by rapid and far-reaching change. However, it might be argued that, in true evolutionary style, the change emerged from features which were already in evidence within the organism itself, and it was shaped by matters in the external environment. In other words, the move towards new organisational structures and a more managerial culture had fairly deep roots within the civil service itself (we traced these in Chapter 3), and was influenced by current and past developments in both the private and public sectors. Indeed, in the context of the public sector, it is possible to discern a process of international cross-fertilisation taking place, between the civil service reformers in Canada and New Zealand and those in Britain (Greer, 1994: 106–17).

While 'Raynerism' and its successors (and even some of its predecessors) involved grafting onto the civil service many of the general and financial management techniques of the business world, the advent of executive agencies and market testing showed that the civil service was responding to the types of innovation taking place elsewhere in the public sector. The civil service was adjusting itself to the realities of the 'enabling', 'contracting' state. In brief, it can be argued that the 1980s and 1990s represented a truly evolutionary, albeit highly concentrated, phase of development for the civil service.

Now, what of the more fundamental question about the disintegration of the civil service? Has the process of evolution simply spawned a multiplicity of new species, while effectively leaving the old creature moribund?

The apocalyptic vision shared by Chapman and some other observers must be set against alternative interpretations. Peter Hennessy, a stout defender of the need for 'a proud, muscular, sophisticated state service', sees the reforms of the 1980s, culminating in the Next Steps programme, in positive terms, as 'a long-delayed recognition that the nature of state provision had changed. Government departments before the Next Steps programme were essentially 1830s technology' (Hennessy, 1993: 3). He expresses reservations about the Citizen's Charter and market testing, simply because they appear to him to have frustrated the process of decentralisation and delegation, not because they represent threats to the civil service as such.

The Head of the Civil Service who has presided over this most rapid period of change in the institution's history is constrained by his office from openly criticising the government's reforms. None the less, the words of Sir Robin Butler are worthy of close scrutiny, for two reasons. Firstly, he has become an active participant in the informed debate about the direction in which the civil service is heading. In speeches and published articles (Butler, 1992a; 1993; 1994b), he has set out his interpretation of the changes. Secondly, despite the constraints of his position, Butler seems prepared to identify the possible dangers confronting the civil service as a result of the changes.

While the service has now discarded many elements of the Northcote–Trevelyan/Warren Fisher inheritance, including the division between intellectual and mechanical work and the expectation that officials should only be recruited directly after education, Butler argues that 'there is a glue which holds the civil service together':

> The political context . . . the public accountability through ministers . . . , the special need . . . for even-handedness and integrity, the requirement for political impartiality, the safeguards against jobbery in appointment and promotion, . . . the public expenditure controls and conventions, all those give special characteristics which run across the whole of the civil service and do not apply in the same form to other professions. (Butler, 1992a: 5)

However, Butler is not complacent. While welcoming the range of reforms introduced in the 1980s and 1990s as a necessary agenda for change, he appears to recognise the possible threat presented by a reform process which moves out of control. Consequently, he has set out an 'agenda for continuity' (Butler, 1993: 404–5). It would be too crude to describe this as a shot across the government's bows, but, implicitly, it indicates that there is a point beyond which civil service reform might become destructive rather than constructive.

There are three items on Butler's agenda for continuity:

- 'The need to maintain a degree of cohesion across the service as a whole.' The scope for creating executive agencies may be considerable, but should not proceed to the point where departments and agencies become quite unconnected entities, with no staff transfers or policy co-ordination.

- 'The continuation of a non-political civil service with a shared sense of the essential values and ethics that make our system work.' In particular, Butler stresses the need to prevent the worthy delegation of managerial freedoms degenerating to the point where a grasping culture is created. The nation would be badly served by a civil service 'in which only the bottom line mattered and the means of getting to it were a matter of less concern'.

- 'The concept of the civil service as a career.' A more open system of recruitment and appointment is strengthening the civil service, but there is a need for balance to be maintained, and the career concept to be defended. There is 'no cause to stop growing our own timber, like good employers everywhere'.

The debates about the future role, shape and functioning of the British civil service will continue. As the millennium approaches, it seems clear that the service still exists as a recognisable entity, albeit now more federal than unitary in shape and ethos. While most of the reforms introduced during the 1980s and 1990s came to enjoy all-party support, and party divisions mainly focused on matters of style rather than substance, some innovations, such as market testing, have become more controversial, and may even have damaged the bi-partisan approach (Hennessy, 1993: 3).

It will be extremely difficult for any future government to reverse the most substantial civil service reforms, such as the Next Steps programme, and, indeed, there is no indication that any of the opposition parties would even consider doing so. On the contrary, they are committed to continue the process. However, perhaps the time has come for a period of consolidation, during which the major reforms could become firmly established. After a while, there is a tendency for the management of change to become an activity in its own right. The civil service, like many elements of the British polity, remains flawed and imperfect, but permanent upheaval and perennial organisational soul-searching produce diminishing returns. Apart from anything else, morale suffers when people are continually told that their performance, in a whole range of activities, is deficient, and they 'must do better'. William Plowden has argued that a 'state of crisis' exists in Whitehall, with widespread demoralisation in the upper ranks: 'Disoriented and destabilised by a decade of almost continuous change, many civil servants are now uncertain about what the future may hold for themselves and for their profession' (Plowden, 1994: i). It was in this climate that the Treasury and Civil Service Committee embarked upon its lengthy and wide-ranging investigation of the civil service. The interim report, to which we have made repeated reference in this book, was published in the summer of 1993, and the process of gathering evidence for the final report continued for more than a year thereafter. A sense of expectation surrounded

the work of this committee, but, prestigious though its reports on
the civil service have been over the years, their fate and impact are
ultimately dependent upon government. While government responses to this committee's reports tend to be characterised by
respect for the high calibre of the investigatory process, the recommendations are not invariably accepted or implemented.

For a more substantial clue to the future of the civil service, we
should perhaps turn to the government's own document, the 1994
White Paper, *Continuity and Change* (Prime Minister, 1994).
Again, we have made reference to this throughout our text.

At the time of its publication, the White Paper was interpreted
quite differently by a number of commentators and interested parties. For at least one civil service union, this document marked 'the
destruction of the civil service we have known for the past 125
years' (*The Guardian*, 1994). The Labour Party's spokesman saw
the White Paper as a menu for destroying ministerial accountability and a unified civil service (Norton-Taylor, 1994). Other
perspectives were quite different, and focused on an alleged lost
opportunity. Graham Mather reckoned that 'Sir Humphrey' had
nothing to fear from a 'whitewash' (Mather, 1994). *The Economist*
viewed *Continuity and Change* as a 'mandarins' triumph' (*The
Economist*, 1994), while *The Times* feared that the momentum of
administrative change could be lost (*The Times*, 1994).

The truth of the matter would seem to be that the White Paper
was a delicate balancing act. Close textual analysis reveals sections
of the document which fit neatly into Sir Robin Butler's agenda for
continuity (including, for example, the stress on political neutrality, and the retention and enhancement of a Senior Civil Service based on the traditional departmental foundations). Other
sections bear the imprimatur of ministers and official outriders,
who are, *inter alia*, keen to engender new breeds of senior officials
and proceed with organisational restructuring, while continuing to
cut the overall size of the service. The White Paper has been
summarised as 'a clear compromise between the hardline reformers and the consolidators, but it is also a benchmark, identifying the journey taken thus far' (Massey, 1994: 52). *Continuity and
Change* contains an explicit recognition of the dangers of permanent instability and upheaval. It restates the fundamental virtues
of the civil service tradition in Britain, while, at the same time,
looking to the challenges of the next century, and lauding the

institution's capacity for change. The obvious weaknesses, dangers and failings of the reform programme to date are conveniently glossed over, where they appear at all, but there is at least an implicit acknowledgement that Britain would lose substantially should the civil service be 'reformed' to the point of no return and disintegration.

Future governments will inherit the federalised civil service we have described in this book, and they will make their own decisions about the pace and nature of change required to produce an administrative regime which is suited for the challenges of the times. Our best hope must be that these governments have the capacity to learn from the positive and the negative experiences of their predecessors in the field of civil service reform.

FURTHER READING
A selection

Butcher, Tony (1995), 'A new civil service? The Next Steps agencies', in Robert Pyper and Lynton Robins (eds), *Governing the UK in the 1990s*, Basingstoke: Macmillan.

Butler, Sir Robin (1992), 'The future of the civil service', *Public Policy and Administration*, Volume 7, Number 2, 1–10.

Butler, Sir Robin (1993), 'The evolution of the civil service – a progress report', *Public Administration*, Volume 71, Number 3.

Chapman, Richard (1992), 'The end of the civil service?', *Teaching Public Administration*, Volume 12, Number 2, 1–5.

Davies, Anne and Willman, John (1991), *What Next? Agencies, Departments and the Civil Service*, London: Institute for Public Policy Research.

Greer, Patricia (1994), *Transforming Central Government: The Next Steps initiative*, Buckingham: Open University Press.

Hennessy, Peter (1989), *Whitehall*, London: Secker and Warburg.

Hennessy, Peter, and Coates, Simon (1992), 'Bluehall SW1?', *Strathclyde Analysis Paper Number 11*, Glasgow: University of Strathclyde.

Metcalf, Les and Richards, Sue (1990), *Improving Public Management*, London: Sage.

Plowden, William (1994), *Ministers and Mandarins*, London: Institute for Public Policy Research.

Theakston, Kevin (1995), 'Ministers and civil servants', in Robert Pyper and Lynton Robins (eds), *Governing the UK in the 1990s*, Basingstoke: Macmillan.

In addition, much can be learned about the functioning of the higher civil service by reading the ministerial diaries of Tony Benn, Barbara Castle, Alan Clark and Richard Crossman.

The following journals regularly publish up to date articles covering recent developments in the civil service:

Talking Politics
Teaching Public Administration
Parliamentary Affairs
Politics Review
Public Administration
Public Policy and Administration
The Political Quarterly

REFERENCES

Baker, R.J.S. (1972), 'The V and G affair and ministerial responsibility', *The Political Quarterly*, Volume 43, 340–5.

Bates, Stephen and Goodwin, Jo-Ann (1994), 'Charter hotline pilot "Cost £68 a call"', *The Guardian*, 2 April.

BBC *Scrutiny* (1993), 4 April 1993.

Bender, B.G. (1991), 'Whitehall, central government and 1992', *Public Policy and Administration*, Volume 6, Number 1 (Spring), 13–20.

Benn, Tony (1982), *Arguments for Democracy*, Harmondsworth: Penguin.

Benn, Tony (1990), *Against the Tide: Diaries 1973–76*, London: Arrow.

Bird, Dennis L. (1992), 'Training civil servants: some reflections after 17 years', *Public Policy and Administration*, Volume 7, Number 2 (Summer), 70–9.

Birkinshaw, Patrick (1993), '"I only ask for information" – the White Paper on open government', *Public Law* (Winter), 557–68.

Blackstone, Tessa (1979), 'Helping ministers do a better job', *New Society*, 19 July.

Bowen, D.E. and Schneider, B. (1988), 'Services marketing and management: implications for organisational behaviour', *Research in Organisational Behaviour*, Volume 10, 43–80.

Brereton, Don (1992), 'From scrutinies to market testing: the work of the Efficiency Unit', *Public Policy and Administration*, Volume 7, Number 3, 71–4.

Brown, Colin (1992), 'Whitehall sacking is blamed on Oxbridge factor', *The Independent*, 23 July.

Butler, Sir Robin (1992a), 'The future of the civil service', *Public Policy and Administration*, Volume 7, Number 2, 1–10.

Butler, Sir Robin (1992b), 'Lure of the private life for public servants', *The Guardian*, 12 September.

Butler, Sir Robin (1993), 'The evolution of the civil service – a progress report', *Public Administration*, Volume 71, Number 3, 395–406.

Butler, Sir Robin (1994a), Evidence to the Inquiry into Exports of Defence Equipment and Dual Use Goods to Iraq (Scott Inquiry), Day 62, 9 February, 53–7.

Butler, Sir Robin (1994b), 'New structure, same tradition', *Parliamentary Brief*, Volume 2, Number 10 (July–August), 47–9.

Cabinet Office (1992), *Questions of Procedure for Ministers*, May.

Carter, Neil and Greer, Patricia (1993), 'Evaluating agencies: Next Steps and performance indicators', *Public Administration*, Volume 71, Number 3, 407–16.

Chancellor of the Duchy of Lancaster (1992), *The Next Steps Agencies Review 1992*, Cmnd 2111, Session 1992–3.

Chancellor of the Duchy of Lancaster (1993), *Next Steps Agencies in Government Review 1993*, Cmnd 2430, Session 1993–4.

Chandler, J.A. (1990), 'The United States', in J.E. Kingdom (ed.), *The Civil Service in Liberal Democracies: An introductory survey*, London: Routledge.

Chapman, Leslie (1978), *Your Disobedient Servant*, London: Chatto and Windus.

Chapman, Richard A. (1991), 'New arrangements for recruitment to the British civil service: cause for concern', *Public Policy and Administration*, Volume 6, Number 3, 1–6.

Chapman, Richard A. (1992), 'The end of the civil service?', *Teaching Public Administration*, Volume 12, Number 2, 1–5.

Chester, Norman (1981), 'Question in the House', in S.A. Walkland and M. Ryle (eds), *The Commons Today*, Glasgow: Fontana.

Chipperfield, Sir Geoffrey (1994), 'The civil servant's duty', *Essex Papers in Politics and Government Number 95*, Colchester: University of Essex.

Citizen's Charter (1991), Cmnd 1599, Session 1990–1.

Citizen's Charter (1992), *First Report, 1992*, Cmnd 2101, Session 1992–3.

Citizen's Charter (1994), *Second Report, 1994*, Cmnd 2540, Session 1993–94.

Civil Service College (1989), *Civil Service College Executive Agency, Framework Document*.

Civil Service College (1994), *European and International Relations Training, 1994 to 1995*.

Civil Service Commissioners (1991), *124th Report of the Civil Service Commissioners to HM the Queen for the Period 1 January 1990 to 31 March 1991*.

Civil Service Commissioners (1992), *125th Report of the Civil Service Commissioners to HM the Queen for the Period 1 April 1991 to 31 March 1992*.

Civil Service Commissioners (1993), *126th Report of the Civil Service Commissioners to HM the Queen for the Period 1 April 1992 to 31 March 1993*.

Clark, Alan (1993), *Diaries*, London: Weidenfeld and Nicolson.

Clarke, Michael (1990), 'Britain and the EC. How Britain has adapted', *Contemporary Record*, Volume 3, Number 3, 27–9.

Clifford, Chris (1993), 'The Citizen's Charter, quality and the civil service', Paper Presented to the Annual Conference of the Political Studies Association of the UK, University of Leicester, April.

Committee of Public Accounts (1986), *The Rayner Scrutiny Programmes, 1979 to 1983*, 39th Report, 1985–6, HC 365.

Committee of Public Accounts (1993), *Payment of Legal Expenses Incurred by the Chancellor of the Exchequer*, 25th Report, 1992–3, HC, 386.

Cripps, Yvonne (1983), 'Disclosure in the public interest: the predicament of the public sector employee', *Public Law* (Winter), 600–33.

Crossman, Richard (1966), HC Deb 5s 734 1966–7.

Crossman, Richard (1976), *The Diaries of a Cabinet Minister*, Volume 2, London: Hamilton and Cape.

Davies, Anne and Willman, John (1991), *What Next? Agencies, departments and the Civil Service*, London: Institute for Public Policy Research.

Dowding, Keith (1993), 'Managing the civil service', in Richard Maidment and Grahame Thompson (eds), *Managing the UK*, London: Sage/Open University Press.

Drewry, Gavin (1988a), 'Legislation', in M. Ryle and P.G. Richards (eds), *The Commons Under Scrutiny*, London: Routledge.

Drewry, Gavin (ed.) (1988b), *The New Select Committees: A study of the 1979 reforms*, 2nd edn, Oxford: Clarendon Press.

Drewry, Gavin (1988c), 'Forward from FMI: "The Next Steps"', *Public Law* (Winter), 505–15.

Drewry, Gavin and Butcher, Tony (1991), *The Civil Service Today*, 2nd edn, Oxford: Basil Blackwell.

The Economist (1994), 'Mandarins on their guard', 16 July.

Efficiency Unit (1985), *Making Things Happen: A report on the implementation of government efficiency scrutinies*, London: HMSO.

Efficiency Unit (1988), *Improving Management in Government: The Next Steps*, London: HMSO.

Efficiency Unit (1991), *Making the Most of Next Steps: The management of ministers' departments and their executive agencies*, London: HMSO.

Finer, Herman (1941), 'Administrative responsibility in democratic government', *Public Administration Review*, Volume 1.

First Division Association (1990), *Life in the Fast Stream: An alternative guide to careers in the civil service*, London: FDA.

First Division Association (1992), 'Market testing', *FDA News*, Volume 12, Number 10 (November), 1–6.

First Division Association (1993a), 'Privatisation plans', *FDA News*, Volume 13, Number 1 (January), 1.

First Division Association (1993b), 'Market testing', *FDA News*, Volume 13, Number 2 (February), 1.

Flegman, Vilna (1980), 'The Public Accounts Committee: a successful select committee', *Parliamentary Affairs*, Volume 33, 166–72.

Flegman, Vilna (1985), *Public Expenditure and Select Committees of the House of Commons*, Aldershot: Gower.

Franklin, Mark and Norton, Philip (eds) (1993), *Parliamentary Questions*, Oxford: Oxford University Press.

Friedrich, Carl Joachim (1940), 'Public policy and the nature of administrative responsibility', in C.J. Friedrich and E.S. Mason (eds), *Public Policy*, Cambridge, Mass.: Harvard University Press.

Fulton, John, Lord (1968), *The Civil Service*, Fulton Report, Cmnd 3638, Session 1968–9.

Garrett, John (1992), *Westminster: Does Parliament work?*, London: Victor Gollancz.

George, Stephen (1990), *An Awkward Partner: Britain in the European Community*, Oxford: Oxford University Press.

George, Stephen (1991), *Britain and European Integration Since 1945*, Oxford: Blackwell.

Gilbert, Martin (1976), *Winston S. Churchill*, Volume 5: *1922–39*, London: Heinemann.

Grant, Wyn (1989), *Pressure Groups, Politics and Democracy in Britain*, London: Philip Allan.

Greer, Patricia (1992), 'The Next Steps initiative: the transformation of Britain's civil service', *The Political Quarterly*, Volume 63, Number 2, 222–7.

Greer, Patricia (1994), *Transforming Central Government: The Next Steps initiative*, Buckingham: Open University Press.

Gregory, Roy (1982), 'The select committee on the Parliamentary Commissioner for Administration 1967–1980', *Public Law* (Spring), 49–88.

Gregory, Roy and Hutchesson, Peter (1975), *The Parliamentary Ombudsman*, London: Allen and Unwin.

Gregory, Roy and Pearson, Jane (1992), 'The Parliamentary Ombudsman after twenty five years', *Public Administration*, Volume 70, Number 4, 469–98.

The Guardian (1993), 'MPs to see film of mandarins' ruses', 24 April.

The Guardian (1994), 'Very civil reforms of the civil service', 14 July.

Hadfield, Greg and Reeve, Simon (1993), 'Civil servants multiply with all mod cons', *Sunday Times*, 19 September.

Harris, Robert (1991), *Good And Faithful Servant*, London: Faber.

Harrow, Jenny and Talbot, Colin (1993), 'The Citizen's Charter', in Christopher Trinder and Peter Jackson (eds), *The Public Services Yearbook 1993*, London: Chapman and Hall.

Headey, Bruce (1974), *British Cabinet Ministers*, London: Allen and Unwin.

Hencke, David (1993), 'Job tenders rile Whitehall', *The Guardian*, 26 January.

Hencke, David (1994), 'Lilley and Heseltine top the league in payments to market-test advisers', *The Guardian*, 6 August.

Hennessy, Peter (1988), 'Mrs Thatcher's poodle? The civil service since 1979', *Contemporary Record*, Volume 2, Number 2, 2–4.

Hennessy, Peter (1989a), *Whitehall*, London: Secker and Warburg.

Hennessy, Peter (1989b), 'Why new masters could mean wholesale change', *The Independent*, 9 January.

Hennessy, Peter (1993), 'Questions of ethics for government', *FDA News*, Volume 13, Number 1 (January), 3–5.

Hennessy, Peter and Coates, Simon (1992), 'Bluehall SW1?', *Strathclyde Analysis Paper Number 11*, Glasgow: University of Strathclyde.

Hennessy, Peter and Hague, Douglas (1985), 'How Adolf Hitler reformed Whitehall', *Strathclyde Papers on Government and Politics Number 41*, Glasgow: University of Strathclyde.

Hennessy, Peter and Smith, Frank (1992), 'Teething the watchdogs: Parliament, government and accountability', *Strathclyde Analysis Paper Number 7*, Glasgow, University of Strathclyde.

Hinton, Peter (1993), 'Quality', in John Wilson and Peter Hinton (eds), *Public Services and the 1990s: Issues in public service finance and management*, Eastham: Tudor.

HMSO (1993a), *The Security Service*.

HMSO (1993b), *Central Intelligence Machinery*.

HM Treasury (1985), *Government Observations on the Eighth Report from the Treasury and Civil Service Committee, 1983–84*, Cmnd 9465, Session 1984–5.

HM Treasury (1992a), *Civil Service Statistics, 1992 Edition*, London: HMSO.

HM Treasury (1992b), *Executive Agencies: a guide to setting targets and measuring performance*, London: HMSO.

HM Treasury (1993), *Civil Service Statistics, 1993 Edition*, London: HMSO.

Hogwood, B.W. and Gunn, L.A. (1984), *Policy Analysis for the Real World*, Oxford: Oxford University Press.

Holland, P.F. (1988), 'Efficiency and effectiveness in the civil service: the Rayner Scrutinies', *CIGPA Paper Number 2*, Sheffield: Sheffield City Polytechnic.

Hood, C.C. (1976), *The Limits of Administration*, London: Wiley.

Hood, Christopher (1991), 'Do we need a career civil service?', *Fabian Discussion Paper Number 8*, London: Fabian Society.

Hoskyns, Sir John (1983), 'Whitehall and Westminster: an outsider's view', *Parliamentary Affairs*, Volume 36, 137–47.

Ingham, Bernard (1991), *Don't Kill the Messenger*, London: HarperCollins

Jackson, Peter (1988), 'Foreword', in Public Finance and Accountancy, *The Financial Management Initiative*, London: CIPFA.

Jones, B.M. (1990), 'Sweden', in J.E. Kingdom (ed.), *The Civil Service in Liberal Democracies: An introductory survey*, London: Routledge.

Jordan, A.G. and Richardson, J.J. (1987), *British Politics and the Policy Process*, London: Allen and Unwin.

Jordan, Grant (1994), '"Reinventing government": but will it work?', *Public Administration*, Volume 72, Number 2, 271–9.

Judge, David (1992), 'The "effectiveness" of the post-1979 select committee system: the verdict of the 1990 Procedure Committee', *The Political Quarterly*, Volume 63, Number 1, 91–100.

Kaufman, Gerald (1992), 'Privatising the ministers', *The Guardian*, 7 December.

Kellner, Peter and Lord Crowther-Hunt (1980), *The Civil Servants: An inquiry into Britain's ruling class*, London: Macdonald.

Kingdom, J.E. (ed.) (1990a), *The Civil Service in Liberal Democracies: An introductory survey*, London: Routledge.

Kingdom, J.E. (1990b), 'Canada', in J.E. Kingdom (ed.), *The Civil Service in Liberal Democracies: An introductory survey*, London: Routledge.

Kirchner, Emil (1993), 'A third level of government: Britain in the European Community', in I. Budge and D. McKay (eds), *The Developing British Political System: The 1990s*, 3rd edn, London: Longman.

Labour Research (1993), *Privatising the Government*, London, Labour Research.

Latham, Michael (1986), 'A watchdog with teeth: the Committee of Public Accounts', *Social Studies Review*, Volume 1, Number 4, 37–41.

Leigh, Ian (1993), 'Matrix Churchill, supergun and the Scott Inquiry', *Public Law* (Winter), 630–49.

Lewis, Norman (1993), 'The Citizen's Charter and Next Steps: a new way of governing?', *The Political Quarterly*, Volume 64, Number 3, 316–26.

Linklater, Marcus and Leigh, David (1986), *Not with Honour: The inside story of the Westland scandal*, London: Sphere.

McDonald, Oonagh (1992), *Swedish Models: The Swedish model of central government*, London: Institute for Public Policy Research.

Madgwick, Peter and Woodhouse, Diana (1989), 'The Westland affair: helicopter crashes into British constitution', *Social Studies Review*, Volume 4, Number 4, 156–63.

Madgwick, Peter and Woodhouse, Diana (1993), 'The British Constitution: ISBN 0 7115 0233 1', *Talking Politics*, Volume 6, Number 1, 36–41.

Marsh, James W. (1985), 'Representational changes: the constituency MP', in P. Norton (ed.), *Parliament in the 1980s*, Oxford: Blackwell.

Massey, Andrew (1994), 'Old wine in new bottles', *Parliamentary Brief*, Volume 2, Number 10 (July–August), 52–3.

Mather, Graham (1994), 'Nothing to fear, Sir Humphrey', *The Times*, 14 July.

Maudling, Reginald (1972), *Vehicle and General Debate*, HC Debs 5s 836 1971–2 c.159.

Maxwell Fyfe, Sir David (1954), *Crichel Down Debate*, HC Debs 5s 530 1953–4 c.1285–7.

Mayne, John (1993), 'Public power outside government?', *The Political Quarterly*, Volume 64, Number 3, 327–35.

Metcalf, Les and Richards, Sue (1990), *Improving Public Management*, London: Sage.

National Audit Office (1986), *The Rayner Scrutiny Programmes 1979 to 1983*, HC 322, 1985–6.

Neville-Jones, Pauline (1983), 'The continental *cabinet* system: the effects of transferring it to the United Kingdom', *The Political Quarterly*, Volume 54, Number 3, 232–42.

Next Steps Team (1993a), *Briefing Note*, 5 August 1993.

Next Steps Team (1993b), *Briefing Note*, 15 October 1993.

Next Steps Team (1994), *Briefing Note*, 1 July 1994.

Northcote, Stafford and Trevelyan, Charles (1854), *Report on the Organisation of the Permanent Civil Service*, Parliamentary Paper 1713.

Norton, Philip (1981), *The Commons in Perspective*, Oxford: Martin Robertson.

Norton, Philip (1993), *Does Parliament Matter?*, Hemel Hempstead: Harvester Wheatsheaf.

Norton-Taylor, Richard (1993), 'Civil servants call for code to stop ministers "passing the buck"', *The Guardian*, 16 November.

Norton-Taylor, Richard (1994), 'Civil service principles "under threat"', *The Guardian*, 14 July.

Nugent, Neill (1993), 'The European dimension', in Patrick Dunleavy, Andrew Gamble, Ian Holliday and Gillian Peele (eds), *Developments in British Politics 4*, Basingstoke: Macmillan.

Oates, Graham (1988), 'The FMI in central government', in Public Finance and Accountancy, *The Financial Management Initiative*, London: CIPFA.

O'Hagan, Charles (1991), 'Come in, oh Conservative Caliban, your time is up', *The Guardian*, 11 February.

Oliver, Dawn (1991), *Government in the United Kingdom: The search for accountability, effectiveness and citizenship*, Milton Keynes: Open University Press.

Osborne, David and Gaebler, Ted (1993), *Reinventing Government: How the entrepreneurial spirit is transforming the public sector*, Reading Mass.: Addison Wesley.

O'Toole, Barry (1993), 'Permanent secretaries, open competition and the future of the civil service', *Public Policy and Administration*, Volume 8, Number 3 (Winter), 1–3.

Page, Edward C. (1992), *Political Authority and Bureaucratic Power*, 2nd edn, Hemel Hempstead: Harvester Wheatsheaf.

Pallister, David and Norton-Taylor, Richard (1992a), 'Concern grows over "revolving door"', *The Guardian*, 9 September.

Pallister, David and Norton-Taylor, Richard (1992b), 'MPs attack jobs for civil servants', *The Guardian*, 10 September.

Parliamentary Commissioner for Administration (1968), *Sachsenhausen*, 3rd Report 1967–8, HC 54.

Parliamentary Commissioner for Administration (1974), *Invalid Carriages*, 6th Report 1974–5, HC 529.

Parliamentary Commissioner for Administration (1975a), *Television Licences*, 7th Report 1974–5, HC 680.

Parliamentary Commissioner for Administration (1975b), *Court Line*, 5th Report 1974–5, HC 498.

Parliamentary Commissioner for Administration (1989), *The Barlow Clowes Affair*, 1st Report 1989–90, HC 76.

Parliamentary Commissioner for Administration (1993), *Annual Report for 1992*, 5th Report 1992–3, HC 569.

Parliamentary Commissioner for Administration (1994), *Annual Report for 1993*, 3rd Report 1993–4, HC 290.

Peters, T. (1987), *Thriving on Chaos*, New York: Harper and Row.

Peters. T. and Austin, N. (1985), *A Passion For Excellence*, New York: Harper and Row.

Peters, T. and Waterman, L. (1982), *In Search of Excellence*, New York: Harper and Row.

Plowden Report (1961), *Control of Public Expenditure*, Cmnd 1432.

Plowden, William (1994), *Ministers and Mandarins*, London: Institute for Public Policy Research.

Pollitt, Christopher (1990), 'Doing business in the temple? Managers and quality assurance in the public services', *Public Administration*, Volume 68, Number 4, 435–52.

Ponting, Clive (1985), *The Right to Know: The inside story of the Belgrano affair*, London: Sphere.

Ponting, Clive (1986), *Whitehall: Tragedy and farce*, London: Sphere.

Ponting, Clive (1989), *Whitehall: Changing the old guard*, London: Unwin.

Ponting, Clive (1990), *Secrecy in Britain*, Oxford: Basil Blackwell.

Price Waterhouse (1991), *Executive Agencies, Facts and Trends Edition 3*, London: Price Waterhouse.

Price Waterhouse (1992), *Executive Agencies, Facts and Trends Edition 4*, London: Price Waterhouse.

Prime Minister (1991), *Improving Management in Government: The Next Steps agencies review 1991*, Cmnd 1760, Session 1991–2.

Prime Minister (1994), *The Civil Service: Continuity and change*, Cmnd 2627, Session 1993–4.

Pyper, Robert (1984), 'Whitehall in the 1980s: prescriptions and prospects', *Teaching Politics*, Volume 13, Number 3, 376–91.

Pyper, Robert (1985), 'Sarah Tisdall, Ian Willmore and the Civil Servant's "Right to Leak"', *The Political Quarterly*, Volume 56, Number 1, 72–81.

Pyper, Robert (1987a), 'The doctrine of individual ministerial responsibility in British government: theory and practice in a new regime of parliamentary accountability', Ph.D. thesis, University of Leicester.

Pyper, Robert (1987b), 'The Westland affair', *Teaching Politics*, Volume 16, Number 3, 346–63.

Pyper, Robert (1991), *The Evolving Civil Service*, Burnt Mill: Longman.

Pyper, Robert (1992), 'Apportioning responsibility or passing the buck? The strange cases of Mr Baker, Mr Prior and the disappearing prisoners', *Teaching Public Administration*, Volume 12, Number 2, 33–6.

Recruitment and Assessment Services (1993), *European Fast Stream*, Basingstoke: RAS.

Rhodes, R.A.W. (1994), 'Reinventing excellence: or how best sellers thwart the search for lessons to transform the public sector', *Public Administration*, Volume 71, Number 2, 281–9.

Richards, Sue (1987), 'The financial management initiative', in J. Gretton and A. Harrison (eds), *Reshaping Central Government*, Hermitage: Policy Journals.

Robinson, Ann (1988), 'The House of Commons and public money' in M. Ryle and P.G. Richards (eds), *The Commons Under Scrutiny*, London: Routledge.

Royal Institute of Public Administration (1987), *Top Jobs in Whitehall*, London: RIPA.

Salmon, Trevor (1995), 'The European dimension' in Robert Pyper and Lynton Robins (eds), *Governing the UK in the 1990s*, Basingstoke: Macmillan.

Scott Inquiry (1993–4), *Inquiry into Exports of Defence Equipment and Dual Use Goods to Iraq*, London: Smith Bernal Reporting.

Scottish Office (1992), 'Investing in people for improved performance', *Scottish Office Training and Development Opportunities 1992–93*.

Sedgemore, Brian (1980), *The Secret Constitution*, London: Hodder and Stoughton.

Seldon, Anthony (1990), 'The Cabinet Office and coordination 1979–87', *Public Administraion*, Volume 68, Number 1, 103–21.

Select Committee on Procedure, House of Commons (1990), *The Working of the Select Committee System*, 2nd Report 1989–90, HC 19–I.

Select Committee on Procedure, House of Commons (1991), *Parliamentary Questions*, 3rd Report 1990–1, HC 178.

Sisson, C.H. (1976), 'The civil service after Fulton', in W.J. Stankiewicz (ed.), *British Government in an Era of Reform*, London: Collier/ Macmillan.

Spence, David (1993), 'The role of the national civil service in European lobbying: the British case', in Sonia Mazey and Jeremy Richardson (eds) *Lobbying in the European Community*, Oxford: Oxford University Press.

Stott, Tony (1994), 'Market testing and beyond: privatisation and contracting out in British central government', *Teaching Public Administration*, Volume 14, Number 1 (Spring), 36–48.

Thatcher, Margaret (1988), HC Debs 6s 127 1987–8.

Thomas, Rosamund (1989), 'The experience of other countries', in Richard A. Chapman and Michael Hunt (eds), *Open Government*, London: Routledge.

The Times (1994), 'Civil changes', 14 July.

Travis, Alan (1993), 'Howard admits rejecting civil servants' advice', *The Guardian*, 12 November.

Treasury and Civil Service Committee (1984), *The Acceptance of Outside Appointments by Crown Servants*, 8th Report 1983–4, HC 302.

Treasury and Civil Service Committee (1986), *Civil Servants and Ministers: Duties and responsibilities*, 7th Report 1985–6, HC 92.

Treasury and Civil Service Committee (1988a), *Civil Service Management Reform: The Next Steps*, 8th Report 1987–8, HC 494.

Treasury and Civil Service Committee (1988b), *Government Reply to the Eighth Report 1987–88. Civil service management reform: The Next Steps*, Cmnd 524, Session 1987–8.

Treasury and Civil Service Committee (1990a), *Progress in the Next Steps Initiative*, 8th Report 1989–90, HC 481.

Treasury and Civil Service Committee (1990b), *Government Reply to the Eighth Report 1989–90: Progress in the Next Steps Initiative*, Cmnd 1263, Session 1989–90.

Treasury and Civil Service Committee (1991a), *The Next Steps Initiative*, 7th Report 1990–1, HC 496.

Treasury and Civil Service Committee (1991b), *Government Reply to the 7th Report 1990–91: The Next Steps Initiative*, Cmnd 1761, Session 1990–1.

Treasury and Civil Service Committee (1993), *The Role of the Civil Service: Interim report*, 6th Report 1992–3, HC 390.

Waldegrave, William (1993), 'Market testing conference report' *Management Matters*, Number 19 (February), 5.

Walsh, Kieron (1991), 'Quality and public services', *Public Administration*, Volume 69, Number 4, 503–14.

Wass, Douglas (1983), 'The public service in modern society', *Public Administration*, Volume 61.

Wass, Sir Douglas (1985), 'The civil service at the crossroads', *The Political Quarterly*, Volume 56, Number 3, 227–41.

Waterhouse, Rosie (1989), 'Anxiety grows over integrity of statistics', *The Independent*, 9 October.

White, Michael (1993), 'All change in thinktankland', *The Guardian*, 6 January.

White Paper (1970), *The Reorganisation of Central Government*, Cmnd 4506.

White Paper (1982), *Efficiency and Effectiveness in the Civil Service*, Cmnd 8616.

White Paper (1991), *Competing for Quality: Buying better public services*, Cmnd 1730.

White Paper (1993), *Open Government*, Cmnd 2290.

Wilson, Woodrow (1887), 'The study of administration', *Political Science Quarterly*, Volume 2, 192–222.

Young, Hugo (1976), 'How Whitehall's mandarins tamed Labour's 38 special advisers', *Sunday Times*, 19 September.

Young, Hugo (1990), *One of Us*, London: Pan.

Young, Hugo (1994), 'The Alice in Wonderland world of Sir Robin Butler', *The Guardian*, 10 February.

Young, Hugo and Sloman, Anne (1982), *No, Minister*, London: BBC.

INDEX